The Transformation of St Pancras Station

1

The Transformation of St Pancras Station

Alastair Lansley
Stuart Durant
Alan Dyke
Bernard Gambrill
Roderick Shelton

First published in Great Britain in 2008

This paperback edition first published in 2010 by
Laurence King Publishing Ltd

361–373 City Road
London EC1V 1LR
United Kingdom
Tel: + 44 20 7841 6900
Fax: + 44 20 7841 6910
email: enquiries@laurenceking.com
www.laurenceking.com

A catalogue record for this book is available from the British Library.

ISBN-13: 978 1 85669 637 1

Senior Editor: Susie May
Technical Editor: Bernard Gambrill
Designer: Robin Farrow
New photography: Paul Childs
Historic image research: Bridget Coaker
Project liaison: Kit Kaberry

Printed in China

Frontispiece: John O'Connor, *From Pentonville Road looking west, evening*, 1884.

Contents

The transformation of St Pancras is a triumph. It has created not just a new station but a new destination, reconciling to spectacular effect the voices of the past – in the glory of a great historic building – with the aspirations of tomorrow's railway travellers, to the benefit of both. The lessons are far reaching, for St Pancras recalibrates the way we view buildings that have served one useful life but seek another. Listed Grade I, at the low point in its fortunes, underscored the architectural and engineering qualities of St Pancras. Crucially, that valuation takes no account of economic circumstances but gives meaning to the deeper and more cerebral qualities that great buildings confer on the quality of places and the lives of the people who live in them. That is what Listing is for. Listing bought time, enabled the wider world to catch up, demanded pause for thought, and challenged those charged with finding a future for the station to match its power and eloquence. This book is about the building of St Pancras and how that challenge was met.

In one sense St Pancras represents a collision of ideologies; the shock of the new in the engineering genius of Barlow and Ordish's great train shed and the reprise of the old in all that George Gilbert Scott had garnered from medieval Europe's Gothic inheritance. But it would be wrong to assume the two elements of the station were conceived separately and merely pushed together; on the contrary, Barlow established the articulation of the whole, Scott demonstrated the adaptability of the new Gothic to handle the practicalities of arrival and departure, the opulence of Europe's grandest hotel, and to meet the Midland Railway's need to express in unambiguous terms that it had arrived in the metropolis.

But by the 1930s the hotel had closed and in the post-war years, with railways in decline, the future of St Pancras was in doubt. For forty years it languished as a backwater terminus, surviving periodic threats of closure as the railways contracted in the post-Beeching years. But all this changed once the decision had been taken to complete the high-speed link to the Channel Tunnel, with a route under the Thames and in through east London. The decision to use St Pancras in succession to Nicholas Grimshaw's interim arrangements at Waterloo was inspired. But to make the new St Pancras work required an elemental re-ordering of the internal spaces, at its most explicit in the connecting of the undercroft with the train shed above. In all this Alastair Lansley's imagination and influence was critical, as was the creative rapport he established with English Heritage and the productive partnership that resulted. Determination to pursue perfection to the last detail, in the face of the inevitable pressures for compromise, has resulted in what now stands as Britain's most spectacular example of an historic building recycled for the future, in this case for a variant of its original use.

As critical to success was the design management of the public spaces, and the detailed conventions that determined how they were to be occupied and run. Again, there are wider lessons for architects and their clients. Had the rigour of the St Pancras protocols been applied at Stansted, Foster's elegant pavilion might have survived the illiterate pandemonium and chaos that desecrates so many buildings – old and new – whose owners have little understanding of what they have or how to manage them.

Alastair Lansley demonstrates here that to do justice to a great historic building requires more than aesthetic imagination and design ability. It requires passion, understanding and determination too, spiced with ingredients of evangelistic zeal.

Sir Neil Cossons
Chairman of English Heritage 2000–7
Rushbury, Shropshire
February, 2008

An inspection team checks one
of the architectural finishes.

Introduction

Designing a major international railway station – the first of its kind in the UK – is one of the most daunting tasks for any architect. But it is also among the most rewarding.

The nineteenth century was the age of the great passenger station. Stations were marvels of engineering. They were essays in controlling the movement of unprecedented numbers of people. Not since the days of the Roman amphitheatre had such issues been thought about.

The railway terminus was the nineteenth century's contribution to the development of architecture. St Pancras International is an immensely complex building. It is among the few buildings in which the histories of society, technology and architecture can be read sequentially – as an ancient scroll unrolling before one's eyes. I was greatly excited when, in 1996, I was invited to join Channel Tunnel Rail Link (CTRL) as chief architect for St Pancras International. I was presented with the challenge of ushering into the twentieth century the largest, most neglected and, I think, the most beautiful of all metropolitan stations.

Old St Pancras station was the work of George Gilbert Scott, William Henry Barlow and Rowland Mason Ordish. To be able to collaborate with them, albeit retrospectively, must surely exceed the wildest dreams of an architect in love with architecture. I was fortunate to have already worked on the transformation and modernisation of Liverpool Street Station where I spent ten years as the project architect.

A transformation as elaborate and ambitious as the creation of St Pancras International must necessarily be collective. I have had the privilege of working with a splendid team of architects, engineers and sympathetic administrators. I inherited a master plan that had been prepared by Spencer de Grey CBE and his team from Foster + Partners. As an admirer of Lord Foster of Thames Bank I have respected this.

I must mention the fruitful partnership my team and I have had with the London Borough of Camden and English Heritage. Their experts have worked harmoniously with the Rail Link Engineering team throughout the design and execution stages of the station's restoration. Such symbiosis could well serve as a model in the future revivifying of listed buildings.

I have tried to convey in this book the variegated aspects of culture which an architect must consider – always remembering that railway stations are still among the most significant urban public spaces.

Treat this book as a museum. Wander through it and enjoy it at leisure. Admire the past and think, too, of the future – the second railway age.

Alastair Lansley
former Chief Architect
Union Railways (North) Ltd
March 2008

Dedication

This book is dedicated to the many hundreds of people who have contributed to the St Pancras International station project. Each and every one can be rightly proud of their achievement. It has taken years of inspiration, hard work, skill and commitment to complete the project. This book can offer only a small reflection of all the effort that has gone into making St Pancras International station a truly world-class engineering and architectural masterpiece for the twenty-first century.

Chapter 1
A Gothic Past

To step from a Eurostar train on to a platform at St Pancras International is now the most dramatic way to arrive in London. The station is a magnificent gateway to continental Europe. No need now for the tedium of a trek to out-of-town airports. Six London Underground lines pass through the King's Cross St Pancras station area. Seven rail companies serve it. Euston is a near neighbour. The journey time from Gothic St Pancras to the classical Paris Gare du Nord is a mere two and a quarter hours. It takes under two hours to reach Brussels Midi/Brussel Zuid – 20 minutes less than the rail journey from Euston to Manchester.

When St Pancras was first opened to traffic, in the early morning of 1 October 1868, it was the wonder of the age – the largest iron structure in the world. It has a single span of 73.15 metres (240 feet). This span was not to be surpassed for more than two decades. St Pancras train shed is now the grandest enclosed space to have survived from the nineteenth century. With the Eiffel Tower and the Forth Bridge it is one of the outstanding monuments of the period.

St Pancras appears as stupendous as it did on the day on which it was first seen by the public 140 years ago. The sky blue of its gigantic riveted iron trusses must have surprised early visitors. This was the colour ordained by James Joseph Allport, managing director of the Midland Railway. At night the most advanced lighting technology now reveals the station's supreme elegance. St Pancras is a Grade I listed building in recognition of its extraordinary historical and structural significance. Its recent meticulous restoration has been acclaimed by English Heritage – guardian of England's national architectural treasures. The historical integrity of St Pancras has been preserved while it has been transformed into one of the world's most advanced railway stations.

St Pancras was built at a time of supreme national self-confidence. Britain had created a new world order, with an empire upon which the sun was never to set. London was the commercial capital of the world. British manufacturing seemed in an unassailable position. British bridges spanned chasms in all the continents. British locomotives were the fastest and the most graceful. Even the station roof at the Gare du Nord in Paris was – and still is – supported by Scottish iron columns. The names of nineteenth-century British railway companies reverberate still – like Caledonian, Great Eastern, Midland, Great Northern, Great Western, London and North Western, and London and South Western. Their distinctive locomotives and liveries are still admired. We look back upon the golden age of the railway with nostalgia. St Pancras belongs to that age – as it does to our own – a new golden age for the railway.

St Pancras Midland Grand Hotel from the corner of Euston Road and Judd Street looking north along Midland Road, c.1927.

St Pancras looking north-west across Euston Road, 1870.

Interior of the train shed, c.1890. With a span of 73.15 metres, this was the largest uninterrupted enclosed space in the world. The first train arrived at 4.20 am on 1 October 1868. It was the overnight mail from Leeds and the journey had taken 6 hours, 15 minutes.

Midland Railway engine no.136 at platform 7. A typical MR engine with a
2-4-0 wheel arrangement and straight frames, it was probably the last of the
'890 Series Hybrids' built between 1871 and 1875. The many advertisements
led *Punch* to appeal for clearer station-name signs across the network.

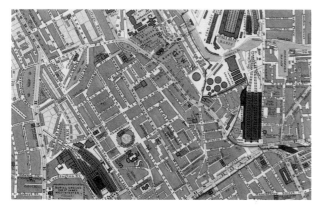

Smith's new map of London, 1860. King's Cross already in place and
the site for St Pancras as yet untouched by railway development.

The Midland Railway

The opening of St Pancras station in 1868 marked the culmination of the
Midland Railway's expansionist ambitions from its home territory in the region
between Manchester, Carlisle and Birmingham. Before this it had a cuckoo-
like presence in London. It was obliged to pay considerable dues to the Great
Northern Railway to use its tracks to King's Cross as its London terminus. The
Midland had also been running trains into Euston from Rugby, but this too was
far from a satisfactory arrangement.

Expansion was a salient element in the Midland Railway's strategy. A route
to London was essential to establish its position and secure its traffics. The
Midland had attempted to negotiate with the Great Northern for a joint line to
London from Hitchin – some 51 kilometres (32 miles) north of King's Cross –
the furthest south its own metals had penetrated. By the autumn of 1862 it
had become clear that nothing would come of the negotiations. Aware of their
likely collapse, the Midland had prudently begun to acquire land in the vicinity
of St Pancras. The Midland Railway board decided to press ahead with their
own route to London.

The London extension was to begin at the company's Bedford Junction.
In a letter of January 1864, William Henry Barlow (1812–1902), consulting
engineer to the Midland Railway, set out an ambitious four-year timetable for
its completion. Contracts would have to be signed and land acquired. Lengthy
tunnels had to be constructed between Elstree and Belsize. Barlow estimated
that lining it would take 50 million bricks. Cuttings would have to be excavated
and embankments constructed. Barlow's deadlines were – almost
miraculously – met.

Horses, grooms, hackney cabs, private carriages and curious children
await the arrival of passengers on platform 5 during the 1920s.

A poster for the Midland Railway after 1892. The Midland Railway began as a modest midland and northern network in 1844. By the time of the regrouping of January 1923, it was the most extensive British railway company.

St Pancras Station

The design and presence of St Pancras station was to assert the Midland Railway's supremacy over its rivals. It was to be the most splendid of all London termini. Philip Hardwick's Grecian Euston, with its propylaeum – entrance portico – and great hall, was noble. It spoke, however, of another era. Isambard Kingdom Brunel's and Matthew Digby Wyatt's design for Paddington – with its hotel also by Philip Hardwick – was magnificent, but, in truth, somewhat passé. The Cubitt brothers' King's Cross was dour by Victorian standards. John Thomas Knowles' Grosvenor Hotel, which fronted Victoria station, was impressive enough, but turgid. On the south side of the Thames, Waterloo was not even in contention.

The site for the Midland Railway's London terminus was Agar Town, a quarter named after William Agar, a miserly and eccentric lawyer. The building of the New Road – now the Euston Road – in the eighteenth century had isolated it from fashionable Bloomsbury.

Frederick Smeeton Williams in his *The Midland Railway: Its Rise and Progress* provides us with a colourful account of the coming of the Midland Railway and explains the rationale of St Pancras station. It was not, as the myth has it, built upon a podium to be in a more prominent position than King's Cross. The reasons for the height of St Pancras above street level are entirely explicable – and ingenious:

Construction of Kentish Town Road bridge, 29 August 1865. The arch centring is in place while the bricklayers complete the pilasters and parapets. The temporary way in the foreground includes a moveable stock rail switch.

Belsize tunnel portal, 15 June 1867. With the tunnel bore complete, a shear leg hoist has been erected to place the stone copings on the head wall of the tunnel mouth within the retained cutting.

Philip Hardwick's Doric arch – the entry to Euston – in 1904, a potent symbol of the railway age. It was destroyed in an act of cultural vandalism in 1962 – despite the powerful lobbying by Pevsner, the Victorian Society and Betjeman.

St Pancras Old Church with tower and spirelets dating from the 1847–48 renovation. The railway works crossed the burial ground, thereby disturbing many graves. In the middle ground workmen construct the temporary bridge over the Pancras Road providing access for building material for the station prior to the installation of a steel bridge and the permanent way.

The alignment of the Fleet sewer with the 'boots' of the iron arch ribs on the east side of the train shed, August 1867. Note the precarious barrow and walkways of planks.

in order to cross the Regent's Canal at a suitable level . . . it would be necessary to raise the level of the terminus from twelve to seventeen feet [3.66–5.18 metres] above the Euston Road . . . originally it was intended to obtain this elevation by making solid embankments of earth . . . the station being bounded on three sides by roads, and the difference being such as to admit of the construction of a lower floor with direct access to these streets, it was revealed that the whole area should be preserved for traffic purposes . . . communication with the rails should be secured by means of an hydraulic lift opposite the centre of the station, at the north entrance. It was also determined that iron columns and girders . . . should be used; and, as the area was to be devoted to the accommodation of Burton beer traffic, the distances between the supports were arranged . . . to allow the largest number of barrels of beer being placed between them. These distances were found to be twenty-nine feet four inches [8.92 metres]. As the great outlines of the superstructure had necessarily to be adjusted to the position of the supports below, the unit of the entire fabric came to be founded on the length of a barrel of beer.

So the grid structure of St Pancras is dictated by the size of a beer barrel. It was said, jestingly, at the time that the station rested upon 'a substratum of beer'. Williams' description is based closely upon Barlow's account of St Pancras, which he delivered to the Institution of Civil Engineers on 29 March 1870. While the overall conception of the great St Pancras train shed can be firmly attributed to Barlow, there can be no doubting that Rowland Mason Ordish (1824–86) played a very important part in its design. This is what Barlow said in his 1870 paper: 'For the details of the roof [I am] indebted to Mr Ordish, whose practical knowledge and excellent suggestions enabled [me], while adhering to the form, depth and general design, to effect many improvements in its construction'.

This suggests the very closest collaboration. It also suggests that the frequent attribution of the design of the train shed to Barlow and Ordish is fully justified. Ordish was one of the most daring civil engineers of his generation. He was the designer of the Albert Bridge, Chelsea, the cupola of the Royal Albert Hall and Watson's Hotel (Esplanade Mansions) – a

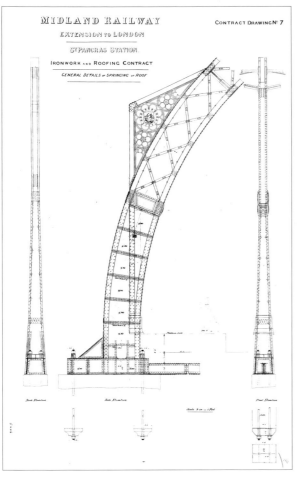

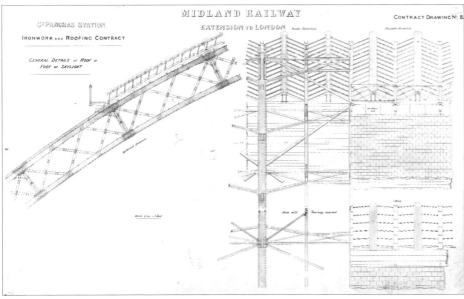

Original contract drawings for the St Pancras train shed. The design was widely publicised internationally and greatly admired. **Top**, arch rib base and, **above**, glazing arrangements.

prefabricated iron-framed building in Mumbai (then Bombay), admired by Renzo Piano, joint designer with Richard Rogers of the Pompidou Centre.

Walter Thornbury and Edward Walford in their *Old and New London* (1880), a popular part-work, supply us with an easily digested litany of St Pancras statistics:

The roof is of glass, supported by huge iron girders . . . forming a Gothic arch . . . It is 100 feet [30.45 metres] high, 700 feet [213.4 metres] long, and its width about 240 feet [73.15 metres]. The span of the roof covers four platforms, eleven lines of rails, and a cab-stand twenty-five feet [7.62 metres] wide; altogether the station occupies a site of nearly ten acres [4.05 hectares]. There are twenty-five principal ribs in the roof, and the weight of each is about fifty tons. The very scaffolding, by the help of which the roof was raised into its position, contained eight miles of massive timber, 1,000 tons in weight, besides about 25,000 cubic feet [797.9 cubic metres] of wood, and eighty tons of ironwork. No other roof of so vast a span has been attempted . . . it contains no less than two acres and a half [1.02 hectares] of glass. The gigantic main ribs cost a thousand pounds apiece . . . in the station and its approaches were absorbed about sixty millions of bricks, nine thousand tons of iron, and eighty thousand cubic feet [2265 cubic metres] of dressed stone.

Top: Excavation of earth from the base of the train shed prior to the construction. This view shows the northern retaining wall of the excavation.

Above: Erecting the cast-iron undercroft columns. These can now be seen in the new shopping arcade. The clerestory of the German Gymnasium can be seen on the top right.

Barlow and Ordish

These figures may impress us but we should also know how innovative Barlow's and Ordish's design actually was. It was widely publicised in both Europe and America. It was extensively covered in the *Encyclopédie d'architecture, Revue mensuelle* 1872–75 – a handsomely produced professional part-work circulated throughout Europe. No less an authority than Viollet-le-Duc, the leading continental champion of rationalised neo-Gothic construction, was on the editorial board. Dutert's and Contamin's immense steel Palais des Machines, built for the Exposition Universelle in Paris in 1889, which had a span of 110.60 metres (362.86 feet), was unquestionably inspired by St Pancras. The system of mobile centring for the construction of the arch ribs at St Pancras was also used in the Palais des Machines. Among important structures obviously inspired by St Pancras station are: the earlier Grand Central Station, New York, 1871; Pennsylvania Railroad station, 1881; Frankfurt am Main Station, 1885; George B. Post's Manufactures and Liberal Arts Building, Chicago World's Fair, 1893; Dresden station, 1898; and Hamburg station, 1906.

Here is Williams paraphrasing Barlow on the construction of the St Pancras train shed roof: 'Under ordinary circumstances, an erection of this kind would consist of two side walls with a roof resting upon them, but in this instance [the train shed] may be described as all roof. The girders of the walls and roof spring directly from the under most foundation, and the iron floor of the station takes the place of ties which hold the whole together.'

Williams quotes Barlow's Institution of Civil Engineers paper: 'A building 100 feet [30.48 metres] in height by 700 [213.36 metres] in length offers . . .

Three-part mobile timber centring for the first wrought-iron St Pancras arch, c.1867. The practice of using mobile centring was widely adopted in the construction of large-span structures, notably the immense Palais des Machines at the Exposition Universelle in Paris, 1889.

The completed St Pancras train shed. Timber scaffolding is in place for the construction of the north gable end screen – one of the earliest curtain walls. This is one of the few photographs to show the refinement of the Barlow–Ordish roof structure. In the foreground are unshaped stones to be used in the station walls. On the right a temporary way has been installed for transporting building materials to the site.

Construction of boots of the arch ribs on the eastern side of the train shed, looking north, showing the holding down arrangements and the riveter's holes, 1867.

a considerable object for the attack of a gale of wind; and being too tightly bolted down, like an ordinary structure of wood and brick exchanges this danger for that of being blown bodily over, like a ship thrown on her beam ends by a squall of wind, or carried up like an unruly umbrella . . . To provide against these contingencies, the same piers, which prevent it from sinking into the ground, are also utilized to prevent it being lifted from it.'

Besides the need to support the weight of the roof – and to ensure its stability under conditions of high wind pressure – there was also the matter of lateral thrust, outward pressure from the sheer weight of the roof structure.

Williams continues: 'In a building of ordinary construction this is partly borne by the walls on which it rests . . . strengthened by buttresses . . . In [the St Pancras] roof the "thrust" is resisted by the solid ground itself, in which the lower end of each girder is . . . embedded while the iron floor of the station supplies the place of ties, and binds the whole structure together. For all structural purposes . . . the building was completed before any of the walls were commenced . . . they are in fact mere screens or partitions...'

As Barlow said, '. . . we have an arch, not only of extraordinary lightness and beauty, but of equally extraordinary strength . . . in point of economy, the difference in the walls [the walls have no structural importance] and the dispensing with the ties give it obviously an almost equal advantage.' Dispensing of the ties – by the substitution of linked iron floor plates – is very likely to have been suggested by Ordish, who had tried a similar method for controlling the outward thrust of an iron pavilion in India that he had designed with the architect Owen Jones. Ordish was also to use buckle-plates for the deck of the Albert Bridge between Battersea and Chelsea in 1873.

Works between the two mobile centring units showing the progressive raising of the side walls between the arch ribs. A workman stands beside the trussed members of the end screen to be hoisted into position. The installation of bracings, purling and rafters has followed the erection of each arch rib with temporary bracing immediately behind the last-erected arch for stability.

A contemporary engraving of the Albert Bridge connecting Chelsea, right, and Battersea, left. Due to heavy modern road traffic, a central supporting pier was added in 1973. The ornate towers at either end of the Albert Bridge, designed by Ordish, opened to traffic in 1873. The view shows Ordish's patented stiffening bars.

The Midland Grand Hotel

The Midland Railway board was determined to match the grandeur of the Barlow–Ordish train shed by creating an appropriately splendid hotel. The driving force behind the company's thrust to pre-eminence was James Joseph Allport (1811–92). He was knighted in 1884. The successful building of St Pancras station and the Midland Grand Hotel was the crowning achievement of his career. Allport was the Midland Railway's managing director from 1853 to 1880 – with a break of three years, 1857 to 1860 – when he took charge of a leading shipyard at Jarrow.

Allport was an innovator – he abolished second-class travel on the Midland and introduced Pullman coaches. During the earlier part of his stewardship Matthew Kirtley (1813–73) was locomotive superintendent. He designed standardised, easily maintained locomotives – always called 'engines' in Midland circles. Kirtley was succeeded by Samuel Waite Johnson (1831–1912) who designed express engines – 2-4-0s and 4-2-2s 'Singles' – that were as graceful as they were efficient. They represent the final evolutionary stage of the nineteenth-century locomotive. Allport, with his energy, transformed the Midland Railway from a provincial network into the most progressive of all the British railway companies.

The Midland Grand Hotel as conceived by George Gilbert Scott – it was to be the most modern hotel in Europe on its completion. One floor was omitted in the actual construction.

King's Cross, and Pentonville Road beyond, from St Pancras station clock tower, 1931.

Sir George Gilbert Scott, winner of the competition for the design of the Midland Grand Hotel. Scott was the most prominent of all Gothic Revival architects. By the late 1860s, however, public enthusiasm for Gothic was beginning to wane.

Sir George Gilbert Scott (1811–78) was the winner of the Midland Railway's competition to design their London terminal – and by far the best known of the competitors. The rejection of his first neo-Gothic scheme for the design of prestigious government offices in Whitehall in 1856 had brought him into the public eye. His subsequent design in a Renaissance style – which was accepted – had brought him fame, if not notoriety. The furore surrounding the government offices episode was the British architectural sensation of the decade – perhaps, even, the century.

During the triumphalist years of the Modern Movement architectural students came to mock Scott's Midland Grand Hotel. It seemed, from the 1930s until the 1960s, naive and hopelessly romantic – representative of Victorian vulgarity and crassness. The achievements of Victorians were ridiculed. Nikolaus Pevsner, an architectural historian who allied himself with the Modern Movement, did manage to find a few heroes among Victorian architects: Augustus Welby Northmore Pugin (interior of the Houses of Parliament), Matthew Digby Wyatt (Paddington station with Brunel), Philip Webb (The Red House, Bexleyheath), Richard Norman Shaw (old New Scotland Yard), Arthur Heygate Mackmurdo (founder member of the Society for the Protection of Ancient Buildings), C. F. A. Voysey (Broad Leys, Windermere), Charles Rennie Mackintosh (Glasgow School of Art). Pevsner had no time for Scott.

Scott's hotel, neglected, became an eyesore. There was serious talk of demolition in the 1960s. But there was also a burgeoning recognition that Victorian architecture deserved to be taken as seriously as Victorian literature. Even as early as 1928 Kenneth Clark, in *The Gothic Revival, an essay on the history of taste*, had explored this incredible phenomenon and surveyed territory that extended beyond the innocent Gothic of Walpole's Strawberry Hill and Beckford's Fonthill. Scott's neo-Gothic was scholarly – scientifically Gothic, even, as befitted the scientific age.

St Pancras International today is a new totality. The heroic age of nineteenth-century engineering and twenty-first-century technology have been brought together and coexist happily. There is no station like St Pancras International.

Euston Road façade of the Midland Grand Hotel looking towards Euston, 1895. Scott showed great ingenuity in planning the most modern hotel in Europe within a very restricted site.

William Henry Barlow, consulting engineer to the Midland Railway from 1857 and throughout its great expansionist years. He was president of the Institution of Civil Engineers, 1879–80.

William Henry Barlow (1812–1902)

William Henry Barlow was born in Old Charlton, south-east London. At the beginning of the nineteenth century Charlton was a prosperous village. Barlow was the younger son of Peter Barlow, FRS (1776–1862), Professor of Mathematics at the Royal Military Academy, Woolwich, which trained officers for the Royal Artillery and Royal Engineers. Professor Barlow was a leading mathematician and authority on the strength of materials and magnetism.

On leaving school at sixteen, Barlow spent a year studying engineering under the guidance of his father. This was followed by three years as an engineering pupil in the machinery department of the Woolwich Dockyard. He later worked for the chief engineer of the London Docks. When only twenty, he was sent to Constantinople (now Istanbul) by Messrs Maudslay and Field – a leading London engineering company and known for its innovations – to set up an ordnance factory for the Turkish government. He also advised on lighthouses for the Bosphorus. He was decorated by the Turkish government for his work.

In 1838, upon his return to Britain, Barlow was appointed assistant to George Watson Buck (1789–1854) who was engaged in the construction of the Birmingham and Manchester Railway. Buck was a prominent engineer and the author of a book on bridges. On the completion of the line to Crewe in 1842 Barlow was appointed resident engineer to the Midland Railway – George Stephenson (1781–1848) was consulting engineer. The Midland Railway was beginning its expansion at this time and Barlow was to play a key part in this. He was appointed its engineer-in-charge – a post he held until

Barlow's piers for the Tay Bridge approach spans replacing those of Thomas Bouch's design that led to the failure of the original bridge.

The south end of the completed train shed in 1868, shortly before the construction of the Midland Grand Hotel. Scott's podium accorded with his secular Gothic principles set out in *Secular and Domestic Architecture*, 1858.

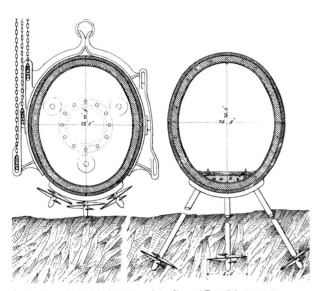

Section through steel double tubes of the Channel Tunnel that were to rest on screw piles inserted into the seabed. Proposed by P. W. Barlow and inspired by the work of his father W. H. Barlow. Described in 1876.

1857, when he was appointed consulting engineer. This gave him the independence that enabled him to take on other commissions. With Sir John Hawkshaw (1811–91) he was responsible for the completion of Brunel's Bristol Suspension Bridge (214 metre/702 foot span), designed originally in 1836, which crosses the Avon Gorge. After the collapse of the Tay Bridge in 1879 Barlow was asked to sit on the official Committee of Inquiry. He advised on the construction of the replacement bridge. He also advised on the construction of the steel cantilevered Forth Bridge. As early as 1858 – just two years after Henry Bessemer had perfected his process for manufacturing steel at a site in Church Hill, St Pancras – he had begun advocating the use of steel for railway and constructional purposes.

Between 1862 and 1869 Barlow was responsible for the construction of the Bedford to London line that established the Midland as one of the leading British railway companies. *The Daily Telegraph* of 19 December 1867 reported 'There are in all 1,200 men employed on the ground. The engineer-in-chief is Mr W. H. Barlow; Messrs Ordish and Lefeuvre have been entrusted with the details of the roof; and the work is carried on under the direction of Mr F. Campion, the resident engineer. It is not expected that the whole work will be completed within eighteen months or two years; but when it is, the Midland Railway will possess the most handsome and complete suite of railway buildings in the United Kingdom.' His roof for the St Pancras train shed was the largest enclosed space of the time until it was surpassed by Dutert's and Contamin's steel Palais des Machines in the Exposition Universelle, held in Paris in 1889.

Perry F. Nursey's paper to the Society of Engineers, read on 6 March 1876, mentioned Mr W. H. Barlow's proposal for a submerged bridge for a channel tunnel railway. It comprised steel tubes carried on piers. The idea was subsequently further developed by Barlow's son, Mr P. W. Barlow.

In 1874, Barlow put forward an idea for recording sound – a precursor of the phonograph. (It is described in the *Proceedings of the Royal Society*, 1874. Vol. xxii. pp. 277–86.)

Barlow was a member of the Institution of Mechanical Engineers, the Society of Arts, a lieutenant-colonel of the Engineer and Railway Staff Corps and vice-president of the Royal Society from 1880 to 1881. He was elected to membership of the Institution of Civil Engineers in 1845 and became a member of the Council in 1863. He served as president in 1879–80. He died at his home, Highcombe, 145 Charlton Road in Charlton, where he had been born, on 12 November 1902.

Rowland Mason Ordish (1824–86)

Rowland Mason Ordish was born in Melbourne, Derbyshire – a large, predominantly Georgian village 12.8 kilometres (eight miles) south of Derby. He was the son of a land agent and surveyor. As a youth he worked in both architectural and engineering offices. In the mid-1840s the office in which he was working was competing for the design of an iron bridge over the Thames at Windsor. Ordish's sketches so impressed his superiors that his design was submitted. It won royal approval. Ordish's bridge was named Victoria Bridge and opened in 1851.

Ordish worked on the design of details for Joseph Paxton's Hall for the Great Exhibition of 1851 in Hyde Park. He was responsible for its re-erection at Sydenham in 1853–54. In 1858 he set up in practice in Westminster with two partners. In the same year he patented a suspension bridge design which he later used for bridges across several European rivers – including the Neva at St Petersburg. Ordish was soon to become closely associated with Andrew Handyside & Co. of Derby, leading bridge-builders and manufacturers of prefabricated buildings for export.

Ordish's Watson's Hotel in Mumbai, India (1867–69), a large and luxurious cast-iron framed structure – with an atrium ballroom – was one of the most remarkable buildings of the nineteenth century. Now sadly dilapidated, it has

Victoria Bridge, Windsor, opened in 1851. It was Ordish's first bridge design. He was 27 years old.

A cast-iron pavilion, of about 1866, for India, designed by Owen Jones (1809–74) and Ordish. Despite his fame, Jones built little and he failed in his bid to design the Midland Grand Hotel. The structure was braced by concealed diagonal bracing beneath the floor level, an innovation of Ordish's.

A cross-section of the St Pancras train shed, 1865–67.

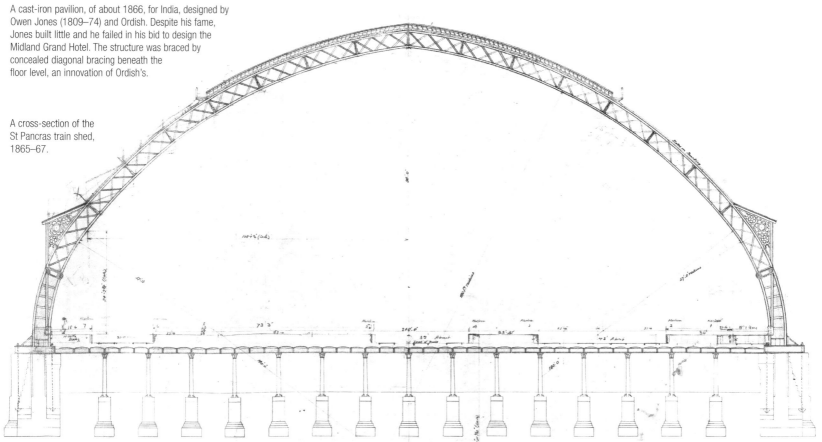

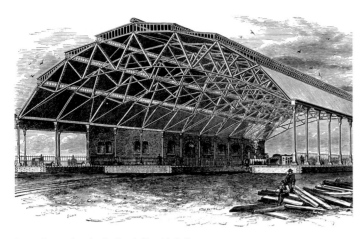
Amsterdam station, for the Dutch Rhenish Railway, 1863, designed by Ordish and his partner W. H. LeFeuvre. Ordish did a great amount of work in Eastern Europe and south-east Asia.

John Betjeman as mixture of crusader and jester defends architecturally important buildings against demolition and incurs anger of people seeking homes in the post-war era. Cartoon by Emmwood: *Punch* 31, July 1957.

begun to attract the attention of Indian and international architects and conservationists.

In 1876, in collaboration with Perry F. Nursey, Ordish devised a scheme for a double cast-iron tunnel to be laid on the bed of the English Channel between Dover and Cap Gris Nez.

Among some of Ordish's more important designs are: Amsterdam station, with his partner W. H. LeFeuvre, for the Dutch-Rhenish Railway (1863); Derby Market Hall (1866); a large 'kiosk' – a cast-iron pavilion in India (with the architect Owen Jones) which had an unusual diagonal structure (1866); Franz-Joseph Bridge over the Vltava (Moldau), Prague (1868, demolished in 1947); the Winter Garden at Leeds Infirmary, with Gilbert Scott (1868); bridge over the River Pruth, at Czernowitz, Bukovina, then in Austrian-occupied Ukraine (1869); Cavanagh Bridge, Singapore (1869); the cupola of Royal Albert Hall, London (1871); and the Albert Bridge, London (1872).

The following paragraph from Ordish's obituary in *Engineering*, 17 September 1886, may explain why, despite his brilliance – and there can be no doubting that he was among the front rank of nineteenth-century civil engineers – posterity has been somewhat reluctant to accord him a place in the Pantheon of great engineers.

'Opportunities he had without number, but he does not appear to have had the faculty of taking advantage of them. He was for some years a member of the Society of Engineers, of which he was president in 1860, but besides that and the Society of Arts, he never joined any other professional or scientific institution, although frequently invited to do so. He had little or no taste for society, which he shunned rather than courted, having an aversion to conform to many of its accepted usages.' Ordish was buried at Highgate Cemetery on 17 September 1886.

St Pancras Saved

Sir John Betjeman, a poet, initially unfashionable in his causes, changed our perception of St Pancras. He, along with the Victorian Society under its founder chairman Nikolaus (later, in 1969, Sir Nikolaus) Pevsner (1902–83), waged a long but eventually successful campaign to save St Pancras from demolition with tacit support from Bernard Kaukas, British Railways Board's chief architect at the time. They may have failed to save the Euston arch, but the public outcry over the destruction of that iconic Victorian structure was so great that politicians dared not risk a repeat. On 2 November 1967 Lord Kennet, Junior Minister at the Ministry of Housing & Local Government, made the decision that granted the protection offered by Grade I listing to St Pancras. It may be said that the protection of buildings of historical or architectural merit needed a champion to articulate their value to the nation; in Betjeman they had a passionate crusader. We are grateful to him. He was knighted in 1969 and in 1971 was appointed Poet Laureate. On the upper concourse of St Pancras International you will find a likeness of the great man gazing in wonder at the soaring train shed roof.

Gas holder guide frames, erected
in 1865, photographed in 2001.

Chapter 2
Dereliction and Decay

Dereliction and Decay

The Environs of St Pancras c.2000

The redevelopment of St Pancras was a long time coming; many years of blight and uncertainty had allowed the station and its immediate environs to slide into decay and dereliction. The King's Cross St Pancras area was gaining a reputation for antisocial behaviour with a consequential lack of inward investment. By the year 2000, before the redevelopment works started, the area was not one that took a pride in its appearance.

Great Northern Hotel from the roof
of St Pancras looking north.

King's Cross station from St Pancras train shed
roof looking south-east towards the site of the new
London Underground northern ticket hall.

View of railway lands and the gas holder group north of Goods Way
from the northern end of the St Pancras train shed roof showing
buildings in Pancras Road to the bottom of the image.

Looking north to railway lands, and gas
holders on either side of Goods Way.

The station from Pancras Road, looking south.
Railings of St Pancras churchyard, far left.

The east side of the station. Left to right: Battle Bridge Road, Pancras Road, Bridge No.1, Goods Way and Battle Bridge Road again.

The west side of the station. Left to right: Brill Place, Pancras Road, Bridge No.1, Midland Road.

Euston Road

On the ever-busy Euston Road the familiar landmark building that was the Midland Grand Hotel announced the location of St Pancras station to the weary traveller homeward bound on the Midland Railway. The romance that had been rail travel, with trains departing to thriving locations in the Midlands from the grandest of railway stations in London, had long been forgotten under layers of grime and the fug of diesel exhaust. No one troubled to look at Barlow's wondrous shed in their haste to find their train in the dim cathedral that was St Pancras. Years of neglect, underfunding and an uncertain future for the railways had led to a spiral of deterioration. Access to the London Underground was through dank passageways where commuters scurried to their destinations and new visitors lost their way.

St Pancras station from above the junction of Judd street with Euston Road looking north-east.

Pancras Road: the eastern flank wall of
St Pancras station from the Euston Road.

Pancras Road

Barlow's magnificent station and train shed stands behind the hotel and is screened from the pedestrian's view by its high side walls. The platforms are elevated to first-floor level on a close grid of cast-iron columns and wrought-iron girders and deck plates, creating a large undercroft not seen from the outside. The side walls are of brick and stone in ornate designs often hidden under the grime of neglect. Along the east side of the station runs Pancras Road, where at the lower level the side walls are arches with barrel vaults behind them that have provided scope for many different usages over the years, from refreshment rooms and offices to retailers and industrial units. As the area declined so did the trade, with only marginal usages remaining. Some of the arches gave access into the undercroft warehouse space originally planned for the storage of beer barrels. In later years, the space was given over to general storage and a taxi-servicing area. At the higher level are the arched windows of the original station offices and, at roof level, a line of chimneys for the coal fires provided in each of the rooms.

Pancras Road: shop tenancies in the eastern
flank wall of St Pancras station.

Pancras Road: restaurant tenancy
in the eastern flank wall.

The further one progressed along Pancras Road, to the rear of the station, the greater became the sense of dereliction, with remnants of Victorian buildings and street scenes; it was an area loved by the film industry, but not an ideal place to live or work in or to raise a family. Amongst the decay there were buildings of importance worthy of saving and reuse.

Left to right: Pancras Road and St Pancras station, Pancras Road again and Clarence Passage.

Above: Clarence Passage from St Pancras station looking east across Pancras Road.

Left: St Pancras eastern flank from Weller's Court.

St Pancras station from Stanley Passage.

Left: St Pancras northern gable end screen from Clarence Passage.

Above: German Gymnasium and Stanley Building from Cheney Road.

Battle Bridge Road, former gas works courtyard.

Stanley Buildings

The Stanley Buildings were erected in 1864–65 by the Improved Industrial Dwellings Company to provide a better standard of workers' housing and were listed Grade II in 1994. There were originally five similar brick-built blocks, two facing Stanley Passage, two facing Clarence Passage and one facing Pancras Road. They were each of five storeys and generally had four apartments on each floor, which have now been converted to two on each floor. One block facing Pancras Road and one facing on to Clarence Passage were demolished following bomb damage in the Second World War. Numbers 1 to 20 form the two blocks facing Stanley Passage.

These Victorian buildings could no longer all be retained, with Numbers 1 to 10 Stanley Buildings demolished to make space for the extended station and a further block removed to allow for the realignment of Pancras Road. However, one block remains and is to be incorporated into the future development of the site.

Upper floors of the remaining Stanley Building are reached by a stone spiral stair leading on to balconies carried on cast-iron columns and beams, with cast-iron balustrade panels. Each flat is entered through a front door off the balconies. Balcony openings, doors and windows are variously treated with decorative clinker-concrete lintels and stuccoed surrounds. There is a communal vertical dust- and ash-chute with cast-iron doors serving each balcony.

Stanley Buildings, Clarence Passage from Cheney Road.

Above and right: Clarence Passage.

Pancras Road: entrance to the German Gymnasium, 'Turnhalle'.

The German Gymnasium

The intriguingly named German Gymnasium or Turnhalle was actually the home of the German Gymnastics Society, a sporting association established in London in 1861, and arguably the first purpose-built gymnasium in Britain. It was built at 26 Pancras Road in 1864–65 to the design of Edward Grüning and listed Grade II in 1976. It is remarkable for retaining roof trusses of laminated timber, which are of the same design as those that originally covered the two train sheds of King's Cross station. An entrance hall led from the Pancras Road doorway (with the door hood inscribed Turnhalle) and passed between 24 and 28 Pancras Road to the central section or western hall.

One of the early directors of the German Gymnastics Society was Ernest Ravenstein. In 1865, Ravenstein and others from within the Turnhalle organised the first National Olympian Games. These were held in 1866 at the old Crystal Palace and on the Thames, but the indoor events took place in the Turnhalle. These events were held annually until the first modern Olympic Games at White City in 1908. The Turnhalle also hosted the embryo British national governing bodies for gymnastics, swimming, wrestling, weightlifting and fencing.

Pancras Road: buildings fronting the German Gymnasium, Weller's Court.

German Gymnasium interior as built with no intermediate floor.

Cheney road looking north
past the German Gymnasium.

In 1908, the gymnasium closed and a long lease of the building was bought by the Great Northern Railway to provide additional accommodation for its operations centre. The building was modified for office use by the addition of a new floor at gallery level. In 1974, the building was let to a variety of tenants, which latterly included an arts' depot with the upper part of the hall adapted to provide space for music, dance and art exhibitions.

In 2001 the entrance hall and central section of the building were demolished along with the properties fronting Pancras Road, to create space for the new St Pancras International station, leaving the main hall, including its south-west gable wall, as a free-standing structure. A new skin of facing brickwork to match the original decorative detailing was constructed in front of the existing gable wall. At gallery level new windows were formed in the existing doorways to echo the windows in the east gable wall, and the existing door openings at ground level have now been given frameless glass doors. The interior of the building was renovated and converted to be used during the construction period.

Further restoration of the building will facilitate its long-term use and preservation of its heritage value.

Above: German Gymnasium western elevation.

Right: German Gymnasium entrance hallway with its dual staircases leading to the first-floor landing, which resembles a ship's poop deck.

King's Cross gas holder station
from Battle Bridge Road.

The Triplet Gas Holders

Another significant feature of the area at the back of the station is the collection of partially redundant gas holders familiar as a notable landmark to all rail passengers arriving at St Pancras. Some of these gas holders are listed Grade II and the development of the new station had to take account of their status.

The cast-iron and wrought-iron guide frames of the original triplet of gas holders had to be taken down and carefully stored as part of the station works, while a new site and alternative use was sought for them.

The developer of King's Cross Central has carried out a number of studies regarding their use and has secured planning permission for the re-erection of the triplet group close to the Regent's Canal, framing new residential flats with a courtyard garden, an aerial walkway, a top-floor restaurant and ground-floor shops.

Above: Camley Basin:
triplet gas holder group.

Right: King's Cross gas factory:
triplet gas holder guide frames.

St Pancras station approaches, c.1900. Three Midland Railway Johnson single engines, turned and ready to take trains to the north, stand close to the water point and its chimney beside the gas holders. An unidentified engine, far left, is manoeuvring a flat-bed wagon bearing a private horse-drawn carriage for attachment to a passenger train.

The Water Point

North of the station stood an elaborately decorated brick building housing at high level a large water tank to supply the Midland Railway's steam engines. As part of the new station works and in conjunction with English Heritage and lottery funding, this exquisite 'Gothic' water tower has been carefully transported from its original location north of the station to a new site. Still looking across the railway, it now resides adjacent to the Regent's Canal basin. Crossing under the railway, Goods Way joined Pancras Road and Battle Bridge Road in a hazardous road junction that added nothing to the charm of the area but provided temporary shelter for those seeking company on a dark night.

St Pancras water point and the triplet group of gas holder guide frames.

The water point in its new location after dismantling and re-erection beside Regent's Canal.

Northern gable end screen of the train shed
from Midland Road looking south-east.

The Train Shed

Inside the train shed, made dark by the extensive use of solid coverings and grimy glass, a pall of diesel exhaust hung in the air and discoloured the surfaces of this once grand station. The shed's two side walls, two gable ends and its arch had been changed or ignored in the period before 2001, and attempts to modernise parts of the space with new retail units, ticket offices or passenger information displays seemed only to highlight the deplorable state of the whole. This was not a station that welcomed passengers into a comfortable environment; this was a place to hurry through.

The side walls had been affected by water ingress from poorly performing guttering on both sides of the roof and, on the western side of the shed, by the construction and then the removal of buildings, which was done with little thought given to disposing of the water. On the eastern side, there was

St Pancras station from the approaches.

Northern gable end screen and north-
west tower from Midland Road.

deterioration in the original side walling when staff left the offices in this part of the station, with a consequent lack of attention to rainwater guttering, hoppers, downpipes and disposal shoes.

The towers at the two northern corners of the structure had lost stonework to corrosion and to a general disregard of the mortar pointing between the bricks, in particular where adjoining buildings were removed for safety reasons and without taking into consideration the watertightness of what was to remain. Some operational additions had been unsympathetic, for reasons of economy or because there was a lack of matching materials.

The glazing in the north gable had been removed; this assisted in the

Above: St Pancras station from Bridge No. 1 looking across Goods Way.

Left: North-west tower and derelict west goods yard.

dispersal of smoke and steam, and latterly diesel particulates, but made standing on the concourse or platforms during winter a distinctly chilly experience. The southern gable had lost its real purpose – to shield the Midland Grand Hotel and its guests from the smoke, fumes and noise of railway operations – when the hotel closed in 1935, and its cleaning and maintenance had become spasmodic. It had been reglazed on its outer face in 1984.

The train-shed covering is the part of the shed that has been most altered over time. Damage to this, as opposed to the actual structure, imposed changes on the pattern of glazing and, therefore, on the ambience of the platforms themselves. The timber walkways and stairways were replaced as

Above: West side wall with entrance to the booking office.

Left: Arch ribs and, **below**, west side wall.

they rotted, but with no sense of the historic nature of the originals. The handrailings that eventually took the place of the cast-iron originals used crude, but effective, road- and pavement-barrier technology.

Enemy action during both world wars caused severe problems, not directly but because replacements in the damaged parts of the station were not properly thought out. Shortages of building materials in the immediate post-war periods led to smaller glazed areas and began the tragic reduction of what had been St Pancras' glory: the sense of space and airiness in the train shed.

In 2001, the train shed had just five rows of glass on each side, concentrated at the eaves and at the third points of the span, with none in the centre or at the ridge of the shed. The poor lighting in the building had been recognised during the late 1970s when passenger facility improvements were

Train shed showing glazing pattern, looking south.

Train shed showing glazing pattern, looking north.

Concourse area looking south-east.

Eastern side wall and former roof
supports in the booking hall.

The booking hall, looking south.

proposed. As a result, extra areas of glazing and additional electric lamps were introduced above the concourse at the southern end of the train shed, with a consequential but partial lifting of the sepulchral aspect of the station.

The sham replacement clock at the centre of the southern gable end screen was an affront to horologists and a lesson to modernisers.

The original booking hall, once a glorious space, no longer had a purpose and stood like a sad reminder of better days, having lost its hammer-beam roof to decay many years before. Its flat soffited replacement with enamelled patterned panels and a lantern area was rarely noticed.

In 1978, the interior treatment of the hall had been the subject of a fierce battle between the British Railways Board (BRB) and the London Borough of Camden. In order to bring the station facilities up to date, it was proposed to

Looking towards the covered way from the booking hall.

St Pancras departures covered way and entrance to the booking hall.

The Midland Road façade has changed through its life. The departures carriage road emerged onto Midland Road through the rectangular opening at the bottom of a steep, cobbled ramp.

replace its linenfold panelling and superlative ticket office with a then-fashionable travel centre and lounge. The objective was to improve the operation of the station by providing better public facilities.

The BRB asked the architects Manning, Clamp and Partners to prepare designs and submit proposals for listed buildings consent. These were refused and in August 1980 the BRB took the application to appeal at a public inquiry. The appeal was lost and the linenfold panelling and ticket office were saved.

The Victorian Society had made counterproposals and in order to make the booking hall more user-friendly its scheme was taken forward. The ticket office was reorientated on to the western wall and the linenfold panelling was reused. This scheme allowed for the improvement of the public space between the ticket office and the platforms. The travel centre and lounge were built behind the south wall of the booking hall in an unused part of what had been the hotel.

In 1869 such a grand station had required that the passenger experience match it from the moment of arrival at St Pancras. The covered way at the entrance was meant to be the start of that experience. The covering was a series of glazed vaults, typical of the Midland Railway's architecture at other stations, which complemented the arches and design of the façade containing the doors and windows of the booking hall. The cast-iron rainwater spouts and hoppers on the wall of the hall formed an essential feature of so delicate an entrance. The road surface of stone setts assumed hard use by horse-drawn carriages and cabs.

By 2001, the roof of the booking hall had been destroyed by fire and the original glazed covered way, restored in 1993–95 and used as the taxi set-down, gave the only clue as to the splendour of the nineteenth-century construction.

Passenger routes into the station changed over the years, and at one time the booking hall was accessed from the concourse, which was used as a genteel palm court where light refreshments were served. At the north end of the train shed, carriages left the station by a steeply ramped and cobbled covered way to gain Midland Road.

Above the former western goods depot fell into disrepair and water was allowed to penetrate the western side wall of the train shed, causing efflorescence on the brickwork.

Eastern façade showing triple blind arch upper storey and dray entrance to the undercroft.

Midland Road

The west elevation of St Pancras had suffered even more than the east side, with fire damage never repaired and a greater air of dereliction and decay. The street was not the outlook of choice for the new British Library, or the residents of the apartments at the north end of the new station.

The majority of the west side buildings were derelict at the upper level, with the ground-floor arched vaults providing a location for a number of marginal businesses, often trading as car-repair garages and warehousing. It was a colourful area, that provided employment and services to the local residents, but it was in dire need of redevelopment.

Midland Road looking south towards the Midland Grand Hotel.

Midland Road looking north-east, the western façade showing street level entrances to the undercroft.

Left: Midland Road, westerly face of the station viaduct. Deteriorated brickwork and miscellaneous signage.

MIDLAND ROAD. N.W

Opposite, top: Railway arch tenancies in Pancras Road at the north end of the station to be swept away by the northerly extension to the station. Left to right: looking north; looking south towards train shed; the American car wash.

Opposite, bottom: Remnant of the Somers Town goods depot standing at the corner of Brill Place and Midland Road.

  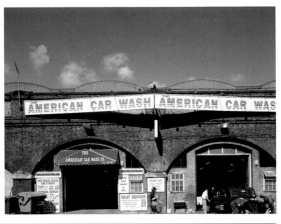

Chapter 3
A New Vision

A New Railway for St Pancras

Planning for a new route to the Channel Tunnel had been ongoing within the British Railways Board (BRB) since the 1970s, but did not gain sufficient momentum to become a reality until after the signing of the Treaty of Canterbury by the United Kingdom and France in 1986 and progress with the tunnel project itself. Initially, upgrading of the existing route from Folkestone, and the construction of Ashford International and Waterloo International stations was sufficient to accommodate the planned and actual passenger demand in the early years following the opening of the Channel Tunnel in May 1994. A team had been established by the BRB in 1989 to find a new route for a high-speed line to connect with a planned new station at King's Cross and link into Waterloo International.

The Channel Tunnel Rail Link

In October 1991, after considering various reports produced by the BRB, the Secretary of State for Transport announced the government's commitment to the East Thames Corridor development and the adoption of an alternative route 'along the lines suggested by [Ove] Arup [and Partners], civil and

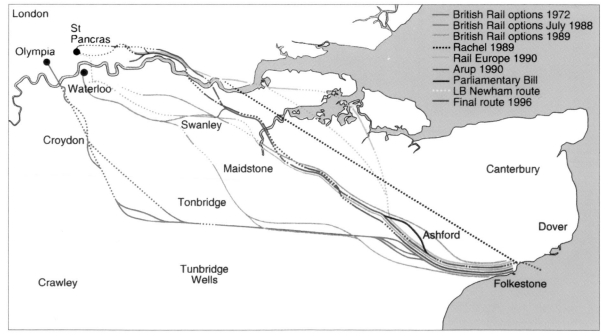

— British Rail options 1972
— British Rail options July 1988
— British Rail options 1989
····· Rachel 1989
— Rail Europe 1990
— Arup 1990
— Parliamentary Bill
···· LB Newham route
— Final route 1996

Routes investigated from the
Channel Tunnel to central London.

Early scheme for the extension of St Pancras station produced by Nick Derbyshire's team at British Rail's Directorate of Architecture and Design.

Model used to demonstrate the extent of the new St Pancras station, 1998.

House of Lords Select Committee at work on the Channel Tunnel Rail Link Act, 1996. *Painted by permission of the Chairman of the Select Committee, Lord Ampthill.*

structural engineers' for the Channel Tunnel Rail Link (CTRL) to King's Cross, via Stratford, as opposed to a south-easterly route being proposed by the BRB. This easterly approach to London had been chosen in part to maximise the benefits from regeneration and minimise the impacts of the line on the environment, including those on residential property. In July 1992, Union Railways Limited (URL) was formed as a wholly owned subsidiary of BR to take forward the planning of the high-speed link.

In March 1993, the government announced its preferred route for the CTRL with two options for the London terminus, King's Cross or St Pancras. It then instructed URL to consult on both route options and at the same time examine the options for the configuration of the terminus and the routes under London leading to the alternative locations.

In developing the proposals for St Pancras as an alternative to King's Cross, a large range of schemes was considered and reported to the government, which included the results of an extensive element of consultation. The Secretary of State for Transport, the Rt Hon. John McGregor, announced the government's decisions on 24 January 1994 and confirmed the choice of St Pancras as the London terminus. The new scheme would include a tunnelled approach through Stratford to St Pancras, and links would be provided to the East and West Coast Main Lines to facilitate through services to the Midlands, the north of England and Scotland; Midland Mainline services would be retained at St Pancras. He indicated that a proposed new hybrid Bill for the CTRL would also seek powers for the advanced works for a new Thameslink station under St Pancras at Midland Road.

The Channel Tunnel Rail Link Act

The CTRL Act 1996 provided outline planning permission for the CTRL, its terminus at St Pancras and associated works. Elements of the railway works and associated development still required detailed consent or agreement from local authorities and a range of other consent-granting bodies or statutory agencies. The means of reaching this detailed consent and the specific works that required it were set out in Schedule 6 of the CTRL Act. Issues related to the environment and historical buildings were covered in the associated Minimum Environmental Requirements, which included the Heritage Deed, a protective mechanism with particular commitments to the restoration of St Pancras station.

In parallel with the CTRL Act a planning memorandum was developed in consultation with the local planning authorities along the route. This document set out the process and procedure for the submission and approval of planning matters. It included the Planning and Heritage Minimum Requirements, which were of considerable importance, not least in establishing the commitment of the CTRL project to the conservation and sensitive reuse of historic buildings, but also in setting the parameters against which the detailed design of St Pancras and its environs were to be developed.

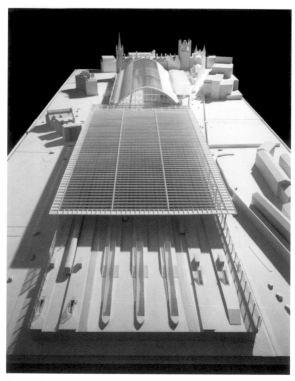

Proposed extension of St Pancras station northern end to accommodate Eurostar and Kent Express services as well as the existing service to the East Midlands.

In order for the proposal to be put before Parliament a reference design giving the boundary limits of the works had to be produced. The principal objective of the design was to inform stakeholders and consultees, Parliament and petitioners of the intended works and to demonstrate a practical and feasible solution for the station, which retained as much as was practical of its original listed structures and character. The detail design was not complete at that stage.

The reference design was used as the basis for the environmental assessment; however, it was also necessary to draw up some assumptions about how the project might be constructed, in order to assess its effects on the environment.

The reference design contained outline proposals for St Pancras station. The Eurostar trains are exceptionally long, and required new platforms in excess of 400 metres (1,310 feet) in length. These could only be accommodated by positioning the buffer stops at the southern end of the existing Barlow train shed and constructing an extension deck to the north of the existing shed. The Midland Mainline trains (now operated by East Midlands Trains) were to be accommodated partially in the shed alongside the Eurostar trains and partially on the western side of the extension deck. In addition, three new platforms for high-speed domestic services from Kent were

St Pancras station inside the train shed looking north-east. The junction of old and new stations showing the Eurostar platforms penetrating the original train shed.

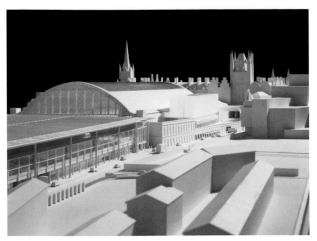

St Pancras and the proposed extension from the north west looking over Coopers Row and Neville's Close.

Sir George Young and John Watts announce the award of the contract to London & Continental Railways, 29 February 1996.

John Armitt, Union Railways Project Director speaking to the press about the decision to award the Channel Tunnel Rail Link and Eurostar contract to London & Continental Railways, 29 February 1996, Waterloo International.

located in the extended and widened station on the east side of the international platforms. The undercroft to the station was designated as retail with the majority of the station facilities being located under the extension deck.

The Search for a Private Sector Promoter

In 1994, the government announced a competition to find a private sector promoter for the project. The selected promoter was to take on the financing, design, construction and operation of the CTRL together with the ownership and development of the UK component of the Eurostar international train service.

For the purposes of the competitive tendering process, the reference design developed by Union Railways formed part of the reference specification, which included capacity and operational requirements, and on which the tenderers were required to bid.

While the successful tenderer was not obliged to adopt the reference design or the construction assumptions, they were required to comply with the requirements of the CTRL Act when it was promulgated, including the minimum requirements. A series of undertakings and assurances given during the consulation and parliamentary processes, were included as part of the development agreement to be signed with the Secretary of State for Transport.

The minimum requirements ensured that any variations made by the successful tenderer to the reference design would be built within the lands defined in the CTRL Act, and that they would not materially worsen the predicted environmental impacts presented in the environmental statement. There were also special requirements in relation to construction and the disposal of excavated materials, and special safeguards for the planning and heritage attributes of St Pancras station.

London & Continental Railways Provides a New Vision

London & Continental Railways (LCR), a consortium of engineering, transport and financial firms, was selected by government to take on the financing, construction and operation of the Channel Tunnel Rail Link, and was appointed as the Nominated Undertaker under the powers granted by the CTRL Act. LCR was a unique organisation in many respects, but particularly because it was established as a transport company encompassing all the capabilities required to create, manage and operate this and other railways; it was not a construction company.

LCR's first task was to reflect on the reference design and with Rail Link Engineering (RLE), its project management team – comprising the American project managers Bechtel, the French rail consultants Systra, and the British consulting engineers, Halcrow and Arup – it embarked upon the challenging task of reappraising the design and planning how it might be built.

London and Continental Stations and Property (LCSP), which holds the property portfolio, is part of the LCR family. It took the initiative and its managing director, Stephen Jordan, commissioned Foster + Partners to

St Pancras cutaway to show the use of the undercroft for passenger circulation.

Computer-generated cutaway exposing the relationship between platform level and The Arcade shopping area.

St Pancras station on the Euston Road looking north-east. The British Library, then under construction, to the left and Camden Town Hall facing the former Midland Grand Hotel building.

assist RLE in the creation of the master plan for the initial station design. Foster + Partners, an internationally renowned architectural practice, had earlier been engaged on the BRB King's Cross regeneration project.

LCSP approached the task by stepping back and considering what was required to operate a commercially successful international station at St Pancras. A key element was establishing a new approach to passenger movement, based on using the undercroft as a vital part of the station operations and not just as for retail purposes. Strategic direction to the design development was given by a clear client brief and a business-driven vision, taken forward by the LCR client team for the delivery of the Channel Tunnel Rail Link: a reformed Union Railways.

LCSP set several central objectives to be applied to the design of St Pancras and the two new stations at Stratford and Ebbsfleet. These objectives were:

- to simplify passenger movement throughout the station;
- to maximise passenger convenience by providing a functional and user-friendly station;
- to promote the railway business of LCR by providing facilities which are superior to the competition;
- to comply with or exceed heritage and planning minimum requirements;
- to integrate the station with the development of the surrounding area;
- to meet safety and security requirements;
- to maximise the business opportunities within and around the station.

LCR, through LCSP and Union Railways, had an overriding concern that St Pancras International needed a defining vision to make the most of the historic building in order to augment the Eurostar service offering and to capitalise on its unique commercial potential. It was felt that St Pancras International should signal the return of the grand station to the UK. There was concern that recent station developments had borrowed too heavily from airport design; but here was the opportunity to develop a twenty-first-century transport interchange that celebrated the best of the past, but with modern facilities to satisfy the most discerning of travellers.

The team was concerned to ensure that the design of the new station allowed for the best possible integration with the LCR vision for surrounding property assets. The LCR property interests included St Pancras Chambers (formerly the Midland Grand Hotel) and the King's Cross development lands. At the time of winning the competition, LCR needed to demonstrate to the government and English Heritage that the outstanding heritage buildings were in safe hands. It regarded the Chambers building, which was not originally part of the overall land deal with the Department for Transport and was potentially

Computer-generated image of the platform level, *The Meeting Place* and champagne bar.

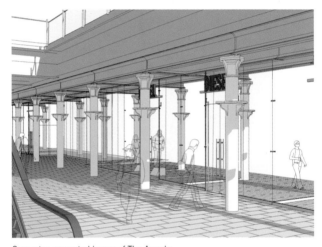

Computer-generated image of The Arcade columns and recessed shop fronts.

Computer-generated image of The Arcade.

a frightening cost burden, as the 'front door' of the station. They quickly committed to a development partnership competition to secure the long-term future of the Grade I listed building. A key part of making the Chambers development financially viable, and hence attracting a new developer for the building, was to create space in the master plan to enable an extension of the hotel to be built on the west side of the station.

LCR committed at an early stage to incorporate an intensive consultation with the statutory agencies and local stakeholders. The design of the station was taken forward in close liaison with the London Borough of Camden, English Heritage and the Victorian Society.

Planning a Twenty-First-Century International Station for London

As far as the overall design approach to St Pancras International was concerned, the brief to the Foster team, carried through by the Rail Link Engineering team, specified that arriving international passengers should experience the grandeur of the building as they walked towards the restored station clock, reviving the concept of a grand station. Also, that departing passengers should be able to see the Eurostar trains. The plan was to simplify passenger movements, provide a viable use for the Chambers building and undercroft, and maximise the other commercial opportunities. In addition to enhancing the passenger experience, it was important that all travellers should feel safe and confident enough to spend time in the station, rather than just passing through it.

The fundamental desire was to make the Barlow shed the international station and create for East Midlands Trains a new station for all their services on the west side of the extension deck; each train operator would thereby have their own station demesne. An additional benefit of this replanning was that because Eurostar trains are powered electrically they are much less polluting than the original steam or diesel trains that entered the train shed, and the restored fabric will therefore remain much cleaner than it was in the past.

The location of the Eurostar and Midland Mainline stations was fundamental to the planning of the new St Pancras. Positioning the six new international platforms in the original station and placing the main-line service on the extension deck created a large area on the west side of the shed as potential public space, in virtual touching distance of the Eurostar trains. In the undercroft this was the stimulus to assemble the international arrivals and departures, accessed via a north–south concourse linked to the south to the new London Underground ticket hall, neatly located below the forecourt of the former Midland Grand Hotel.

By locating the domestic services for the Midland Mainline platforms 1 to 4 and the future high-speed services to Kent platforms 11 to 13 in the extended station, just beyond the Barlow train shed, and positioning a new Thameslink station concourse immediately beneath platforms 1 to 4, it was possible to create a new east–west concourse for all the domestic rail

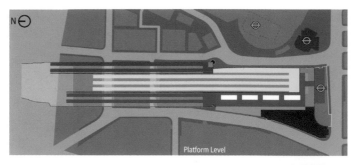

Platform Level

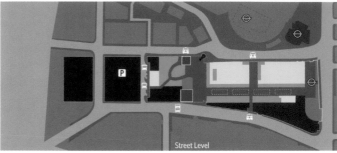

Street Level

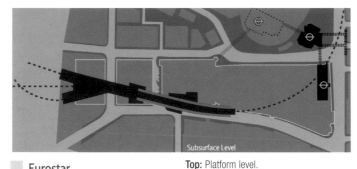

Subsurface Level

Eurostar
First Capital Connect
Southeastern
East Midlands Trains
Public concourse
Hotel
Retail
Domestic ticket office
Back-of-house
Underground

Top: Platform level.
Middle: Ground floor.
Bottom: First Capital Connect platform level.

services. This will be linked at the eastern end to the new London Underground and Network Rail northern ticket hall adjacent to King's Cross, giving easier access to the deep tube lines at King's Cross St Pancras underground station. These arrangements combined with the dedication of the original train shed to international services made the most dramatic changes to the original reference design. Primarily these were:

- to move the main entrance to the station away from Euston Road;
- to cut large openings through the original platform deck within the Barlow train shed in the location previously occupied by the Midland Mainline services.

This was not enacted before agreeing with the planning authority as well as English Heritage that the historic station would be enhanced by these radical changes. The changes helped to solve the problem of achieving a coherent concourse for the whole station; integrating the two levels and enhancing the attractiveness of the street-level space by letting daylight reach the ground-level concourse. Where previously there was a large, dark undercroft beneath the platform deck, large slots have been formed to create a genuine two-level space where users will see and be aware of both levels, and be able to move between them. The perceived volume of the original station is thus increased from platform level down to street level. This has transformed the massive undercroft below the station deck from a liability into a major asset.

The station's new main entrance is at ground level on the east side. There is a commensurately authoritative entrance on the west side on Midland Road, and it is still possible to enter from the south through the original grand archway or the new London Underground ticket hall.

Transition roof between the old and new stations showing Pancras Road and the entrance to the subway connecting to the London Underground/Network Rail northern ticket hall.

Pancras Road is now a one-way northbound road along the station's east side and passes the German Gymnasium and Stanley Buildings. On the western side, Midland Road has been made partly one-way, creating, with a realigned Goods Way, a road traffic gyratory system around the enlarged station. This road layout also incorporates a dedicated taxi lane designed to ease the problem of traffic congestion, common at major city-centre transport interchanges, by providing a space to set down travellers on the Pancras Road side and a pick-up point in Midland Road. New bus stops are located close to the station entrances on both Pancras Road and Midland Road.

Pedestrian Circulation

Most pedestrian circulation is at street level. At the Euston Road end, the main north–south circulation concourse leads directly into London Underground's new western ticket hall, giving access to the subsurface Underground lines and linked to the refurbished and extended London Underground central tube ticket hall.

Fronting this north–south concourse are the international departure and arrival lounges and Eurostar's ticket office and travel centre. At the northern end this concourse joins the east–west concourse located at the mid-point of the station between the main pedestrian entrances and is both the heart of the new station and the interface between the old and the new. From this central concourse there are escalator and subway connections (to be opened in 2009) and Network Rail's King's Cross station. Access to the Midland Mainline platforms 1 to 4 and CTRL domestic platforms 11 to 13 is by escalators, lifts and stairs. Access to the new Thameslink station is from the western end of the concourse.

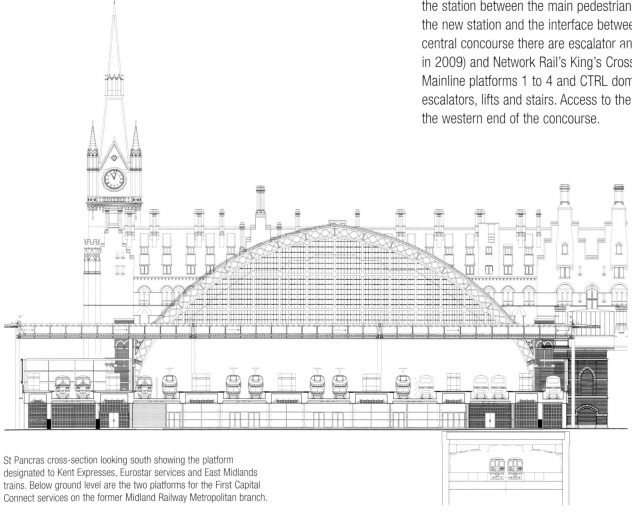

St Pancras cross-section looking south showing the platform designated to Kent Expresses, Eurostar services and East Midlands trains. Below ground level are the two platforms for the First Capital Connect services on the former Midland Railway Metropolitan branch.

North of this east–west concourse and the main retail outlets is a coach station, complete with group-baggage handling and left luggage facilities. Further north again is a two-storey car park, accessed from Pancras Road. Goods Way, the main road crossing under the station, leads to Midland Road. Finally, north of Goods Way, the space under the platform deck houses servicing facilities for the train operators, with direct access up to the northern ends of all St Pancras' 13 platforms.

Passenger Facilities

The Eurostar platforms are over 400 metres (1,310 feet) long, and, given that the platform deck is elevated at St Pancras, the pedestrian concourses across the station help to prevent the building forming a major barrier to local access. For international departures, all the facilities are directly below the trains, with multiple travelators, stairs and lifts to the platforms. It is known that travelators are preferred by passengers with baggage trolleys and child buggies, and these have been positioned at locations that deliver the passengers to the central portion of the train.

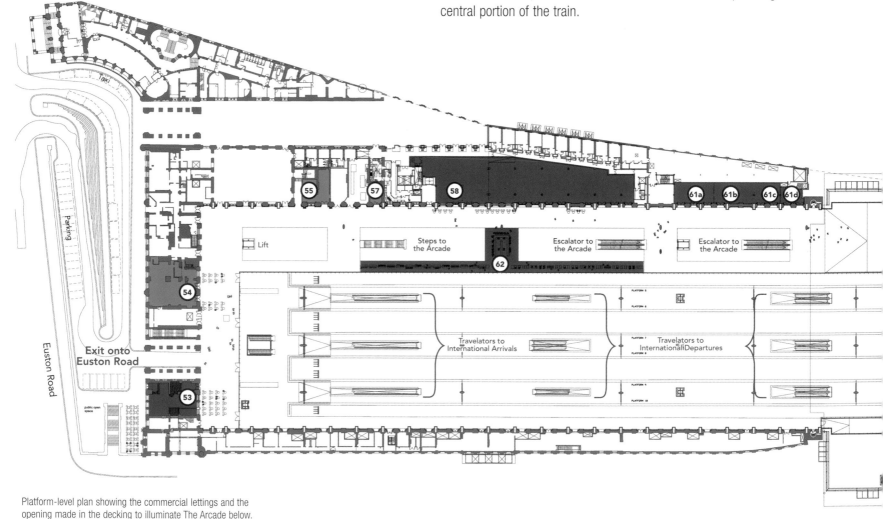

Platform-level plan showing the commercial lettings and the opening made in the decking to illuminate The Arcade below.

The natural tendency of arriving international passengers who are leaving a train at a city terminus is to walk forwards towards the buffer stops. The time they take to walk along platforms from the carriages regulates the flow through the necessary immigration and customs control barriers. With travelators, stairs and lifts down to the arrivals hall provided at the ends of the platforms, it is possible to avoid long queues resulting from border control formalities.

Sophisticated computer modelling of pedestrian circulation was used to analyse the capacity of the public spaces and passenger movements, to satisfy the comfort levels expected at a major terminal. The team realised that for international train travel to compete with short-haul flights, St Pancras had to be planned with efficient and comfortable passenger facilities, rather than the labyrinth of retail outlets commonly found at international airports. It is, therefore, possible to board a train within ten minutes of arriving at the Eurostar ticket barrier line, subject to security checks.

At peak periods the station circulation allows for over 50 train arrivals and departures per hour and is designed to accommodate three international train departures within 15 minutes, two of which are separated by only three minutes. The international capacity roughly equates to the passenger numbers using Heathrow Terminal 4, and this, in turn, is only a third of the total number of international and domestic passengers expected to use the station in the future.

KEY

◼ St Pancras retail let

◼ St Pancras retail under negotiation

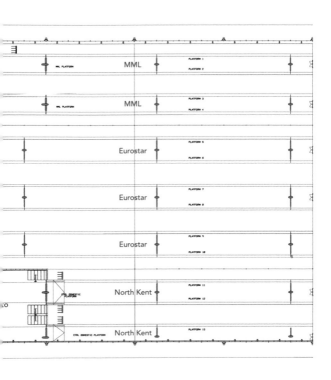

Computer-generated image of platform level showing the slots cut into the deck, 2001.

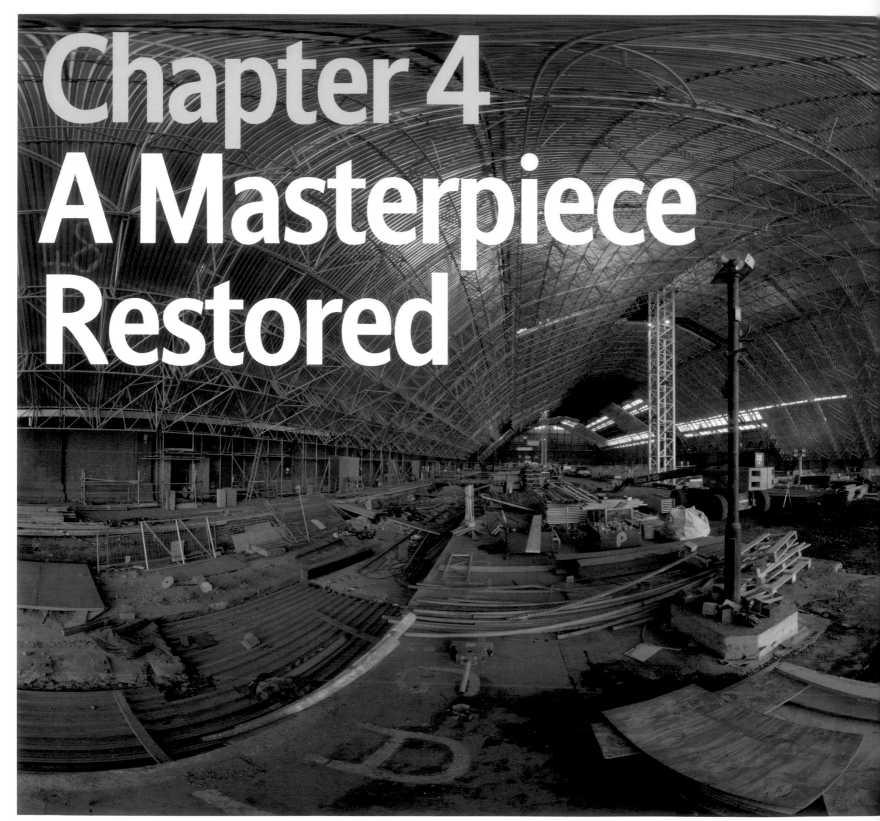

Chapter 4
A Masterpiece
Restored

Train shed interior under restoration and platform
decking under construction, October 2004.

A Masterpiece Restored

West side arch ribs and side
wall in poor condition.

The new station has myriad triumphant achievements, the first of which must surely be the refurbishment of the Barlow roof and its glazing which, together with its transition roof and extension to the north, exceeds all expectations. A combination of the old and the new where 1868 meets 2007 was never going to be easy, but the two languages sit happily together giving further integrity, dignity and, above all, delight.

William Barlow's masterpiece was completed 21 years before the Eiffel Tower was officially opened in 1889 and was, of its time, very 'high tech'. The new additions have continued in this idiom and are wholly twenty-first century; however, where the reconstruction of the past has been necessary, the restoration has been faithful to the original details.

In the overall restoration the arched roof has been cleaned, repaired, restored, repainted and reglazed. The wrought-iron roof structure was generally in better condition than expected, but a number of the arch springing points, known as 'boots', were extensively corroded as were some of the roof elements and gables; these all needed to be carefully rebuilt. The RLE team undertook detailed analyses with a range of assessments of material corrosion losses both now and into the future, in order to determine what was an acceptable condition and where repairs would be needed.

The Barlow train shed at St Pancras comprises the clear-span wrought-iron arched roof with its east and west side walls, the platform-level deck and tie structure, and the undercroft supported on cast-iron columns below the platforms. The train shed abuts the former Midland Grand Hotel to the south and is flanked by the east side and west side buildings. North of the train shed, the railway lines passed over the northern vaults and retained earth embankments before crossing Bridge No.1 above Pancras Road.

The roof was built under a contract of 18 July 1866 with the Butterley Iron Company, which was to supply and erect the roof and also the iron girders and columns of the undercroft. The roof has remained very much as originally

East side wall of train shed
condition looking north.

The south gable end screen and
additional glazing installed to improve
light levels on the concourse.

Train shed catwalk
handrailing, 2002.

Top: Train shed from crown of structure shortly before opening, looking north, 1868.

Above: Train shed roof from the top of the southern gable end screen, looking north, July 2002.

Top: St Pancras train shed roof looking south during restoration.
Above: Roof covering in progress on the western side of the
arch, looking north from the former hotel building, August 2005.

Top: Restored roof structure before coverings were installed, June 2005.
Middle: New roof covering underway in April 2006 with successive layers of
profiled sheeting battens and slating. **Bottom:** Train shed roof slating in progress.

constructed except for the coverings which were altered significantly during the lifetime of the building, mainly as a result of war damage. The LCR obligation under the St Pancras Planning and Heritage Minimum Requirements stated that the refurbishment must enhance the fabric and secure the restoration of the train shed, particularly the roof and architectural details. Thankfully, the roof structure was well documented in the original contract drawings that were obtained from the National Archives at Kew, and later in railway records, which gave designers a head start in understanding the intricacies of this remarkable building.

The Roof in 2000

The existing single-span arch roof was covered from east to west by four bands of glazing alternating with three bands of opaque sheeting, running north–south. There was a further east–west band of glazing extended over the south end of the concourse. The glazing was a mixture of wired and unwired glass, exceedingly obscured by dirt. A continuous ventilator ran along the crown of the roof. This arrangement gave the station a very dark and dismal atmosphere quite unlike the original design.

All the roof coverings had to be taken away to reveal, and allow repairs to, the roof structure which is of riveted wrought iron. There are 25 principal arch members, framing 22 bays, 8.92 metres (29 feet 4 inches) wide, twice the undercroft column spacing, with the north and south gable frames framed by twin arches at 4.47 metres (14 feet 8 inches) spacing. The arches are fabricated as riveted plate sections at their springings from the platform level, opening out into lattice braced top and bottom boom members forming a rectangular open box structure over the greater part of their span.

Top: Interior of train shed during construction of platform-level deck. **Above:** The train shed restored and in the process of being recovered, looking south towards former hotel building from crane above the station, September 2005.

Train shed arch rib and purlin construction.

Western train shed side wall with sun striking the shoulder of the arch ribs where they encounter the side wall, September 2007.

Train shed roof covering at base of glazing with sheeting, August 2007.

Longitudinal lattice-girders acting as principal purlins.

Train shed east side looking north towards gable end screen.

Fifteen longitudinal lattice-girders spanning north–south act as principal purlins, which also serve to brace the arches and contribute to longitudinal stability. Diagonal bracing in the plane of the roof provides further stability in the north–south direction. Flat strip bracing is used in the more steeply inclined outermost panels of the roof, with inverted T-sections in the flatter central eight panels where a strip section would sag under its own weight.

In each bay, there are three principal rafters of curved I-beam section, spaced equally between arch members. These span on to the longitudinal trusses and carry the roof coverings.

The triangular spaces between the main arches and the side walls are framed by wrought-iron members, and infilled by decorative cast-iron spandrels. The top sloping wrought-iron members here carry the roof coverings, spanning between the train shed side walls and the main arch members.

Train shed catwalk rebuilt to the original drawings.

The original roof covering consisted of Welsh slates and timber-framed glazing. The glass occupied the central part of the roof span with slates on timber boarding to either side, east and west. There was evidence of the two original walkways with ornamental cast-iron bracketing and handrails that ran north–south at the quarter-points of the arches at the junction between the opaque and clear roofing materials. With help from the original drawings, it has been able to recreate all these original details, substituting where necessary cast aluminium for cast iron where the element was not loadbearing. An additional cross member and toe upstand has also been added to the original 'infill' between the balustrade and walkway to increase the safety aspects now necessary for walkways at these dizzy heights.

To retile the roof 'best Welsh slates' were sourced. In all, some 160,000 slates of a single size have been fixed, using traditional nails, to treated timber battens. A water barrier of profiled metal decking underlays the tiling supported by new Z-purlins fixed to the main structural arches. Cladding the underside immediately above the arches and principal rafters are colour-coated perforated aluminium planks that match the size and profile of the original timber planks. The cladding contains internal acoustic absorption material to improve the clarity of the station announcements.

Slating of the train shed roof in progress.

Ridge and furrow glazing perfected through research on weather exposure.

Southern end of train shed roof looking
west towards the clock tower spire.

The New Ridge and Furrow Glazing

The glazing was of the 'ridge and furrow' type made famous on the Crystal Palace constructed for the Great Exhibition of 1851. On the restored train shed the glazing has been improved from Georgian wired rough-cast glass to a clear laminated safety glass. A staggering 9,400 square metres (101,180 square feet) of glass has been fixed into 14,100 powder-coated aluminium glazing bars, which match the original timber glazing bars in terms of profile and sight lines. The small end gables to each ridge were never glazed but did have a casting to support the ridge and furrow. This has now been replicated to take glazing.

The ridge and furrow is an efficient profile as it ensures that rainwater drains quickly from the ridges of the glass downwards into the 'furrows' or local gutters. The 'ridge' had also been designed to provide permanent ventilation for smoke from the steam engines but consequently allowed in rainwater. The project team carried out a series of tests on the new glazing under simulated rainstorm conditions and modified the details, closing up the ventilation gap from 45 to 25 millimetres. However, ventilation of the train shed is still an essential element, even though in the refurbished shed neither steam nor diesel trains will pollute the air. In order to ensure an adequate level of ventilation a computer simulation of the train shed interior was made and this confirmed that the revised glazing apertures are satisfactory for a comfortable station environment.

Above: Panoramic view of the ridge and furrow glazing system.

Left: Northern gable end screen looking south west at twilight.

Restoration of the Gable Ends

The gable ends comprise a pair of arches, at 4.47 metre (14 foot 8 inch) spacing, with a cross-braced lattice joining the bottom two curved chords. A cross-braced lattice is also set perpendicularly between the two arches at the location of each of the principal north–south purlins to the main roof. Both gables are in effect three-dimensional structures in riveted wrought iron, the whole acting to resist wind forces on the gable. Evidence was found of the original fixing cleats that captured the original timber joinery and glass end screen placed within the centre of the north gable.

The south gable had been reglazed on the outer face of the gable in 1984. Again with the help of the original drawings, which carefully detailed the infill glazing, it has been possible to reglaze both the north and south end gable screens. Each gable now gives 'delight'; the northern gable, in particular, is an essay in hierarchy with the horizontal and vertical ironwork appearing muscular against the delicate glazing bars. The southern gable takes on a different appearance, with its interplay of reflections and glimpses through to the façade of the hotel. The transition roof between the train shed gable and the façade of the hotel has been reglazed with new glazing bars and clear safety glass, which now enables spectacular views of the external face of the restored hotel.

Above: North gable end screen from below. **Below:** Barlow contained the horizontal thrust of the train shed with a dramatic and complex series of multiple riveted wrought-iron trusses. There is a similar construction at the south end.

Above: Northern end screen with transition roof and extension. **Facing page:** Northern end gable. Gilbert Scott was delighted that Barlow chose a pointed Gothic structure for the greatest roof span of the era. The finials are, nevertheless, Neo-classical.

Above: The clock installed in 1978 after the removal of the 1868 original.

Right: Southern gable end screen and The Arcade from platform level.

Below: Southern gable end screen, 2001.

Bottom: Southern gable end screen at night.

A Grand Station Clock

The southern gable contained a large clock, a 1975 replacement of the original made of glass-reinforced plastic, but the project was fortunate to trace the original St Pancras clock, which was to have been purchased by an American collector and taken to the United States. Sadly, in the course of being dismantled the face fell on to the station concourse and shattered into hundreds of pieces. Needless to say, the sale was off. A signalman, Roland Hoggard, offered to buy the broken clock and its workings from the contractor for £25. He transported it piece by piece, by railway carriage, back to his smallholding at Thurgarton in Leicestershire and, after selecting some 108

Above: Roland Hoggard and the original St Pancras clock, Thurgarton, Leicestershire.

Below: The new St Pancras train shed clock.

larger pieces, decided to mount them on the northern external wall of his barn and render the clock face. He then painted the face in its original colouring.

The clock face and its workings are at Thurgarton to this day. In June 2006, London & Continental Railways commissioned Dent & Co., who made the original, to see if it could purchase the clock from Roland Hoggard and restore it. After an inspection they concluded that to move the clock would not be possible and that the best proposal was to manufacture a closely matching replica. Dent & Co. identified that the original clock consisted of a slate base, stone inner ring and cast-concrete outer ring. The chapter ring had inlaid slate diamond-shaped hour markers, which were in turn inlaid with gilded Roman numeral numbers. Dent's clock face replicates the original in all aspects of the multilayer structure but calls on modern materials in its principal construction. The inlaid diamond-shaped hour markers are, again, produced from slate sourced from the original quarry area of Swithland, Leicestershire.

The overall clock diameter is 5.15 metres (16 feet 9 inches) which includes a 450-millimetre (17-inch) decorative outer ring and side casing, moulded from the original. The decorative moulding is picked out in 23 carat, double thickness, English gold leaf. The chapter ring has a diameter of 4.25 metres (14 feet) and is 830 millimetres (32 inches) wide. Through paint analysis it was found that the original colour of the chapter ring was white, with the black slate diamond markers further inlaid with Roman numerals that were also finished in the 23 carat gold leaf. The clock hands were manufactured to match the original hands without external counterbalances and are fabricated from aluminium finished with English gold leaf. This replica clock was agreed by both English Heritage and the London Borough of Camden, and now welcomes international travellers as they alight from Eurostar trains and walk along the platform.

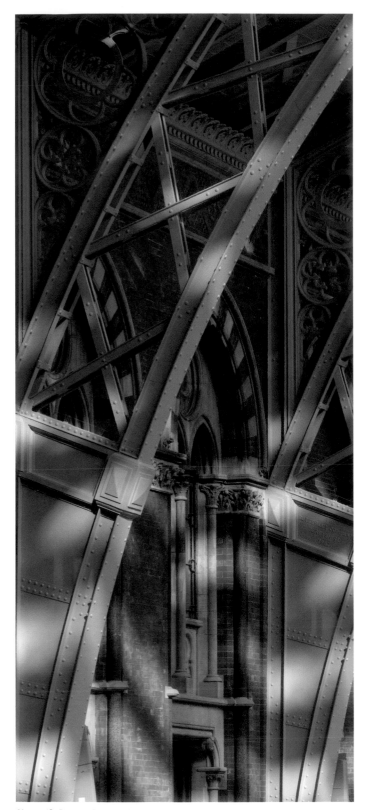

Above: 'St Pancras Blue' against the western side wall brickwork.

Facing page: 'St Pancras Blue' against the sky.

The 'St Pancras Blue' Colour Scheme

Choosing a colour scheme for a Grade I listed building can be a fraught affair with many differing views and opinions as to what it should be. It was known from analysis of the existing paintwork that the ironwork had been painted 18 times before the present restoration and that the original colour was dark brown – not particularly appealing! However, from the records the project ascertained that in 1877, the opening date for the Midland Grand Hotel, the Midland's managing director, James Allport, had asked, 'Why cannot the train shed be the colour of the sky?' Research found that the second coat of paint was indeed sky blue. There are no contemporary records that specifically describe the implementation of the decoration although both published accounts and archival documents reveal that colour was indeed a matter of some debate at the time the station was opened, with differing views from Barlow, Allport and Gilbert Scott.

Barlow's reported post-construction account of the rationale for the roof colour would seem to indicate that he had deliberately chosen a dark one so as not to reveal the dirt build-up within the station. Allport, however, disagreed and expressed his unhappiness at the time in a debate at the Institution of Civil Engineers, where he said of the choice of colour that it made the station 'look exceedingly dull and heavy and marred, to some extent, the grand appearance which the station would have otherwise have exhibited'.

It is Allport's 'colour of the sky' that now adorns the ironwork. It has to be said that on a sunny day the blue comes into its own and blends into 'the colour of the sky' with two additional components. One is the numerous shadows cast by the glazing bars of the restored ridge and furrow glazing, and the other is the yellow effect from the sun itself. If the rest of the surrounding shed is shaded out, the pattern is better than any Highland clan tartan – perhaps it should be named the 'Barlow/Ordish Tartan'. It would be appropriate if the blue was maintained and became known as 'St Pancras Blue', in the same way that the great railway companies were known for their distinctive liveries.

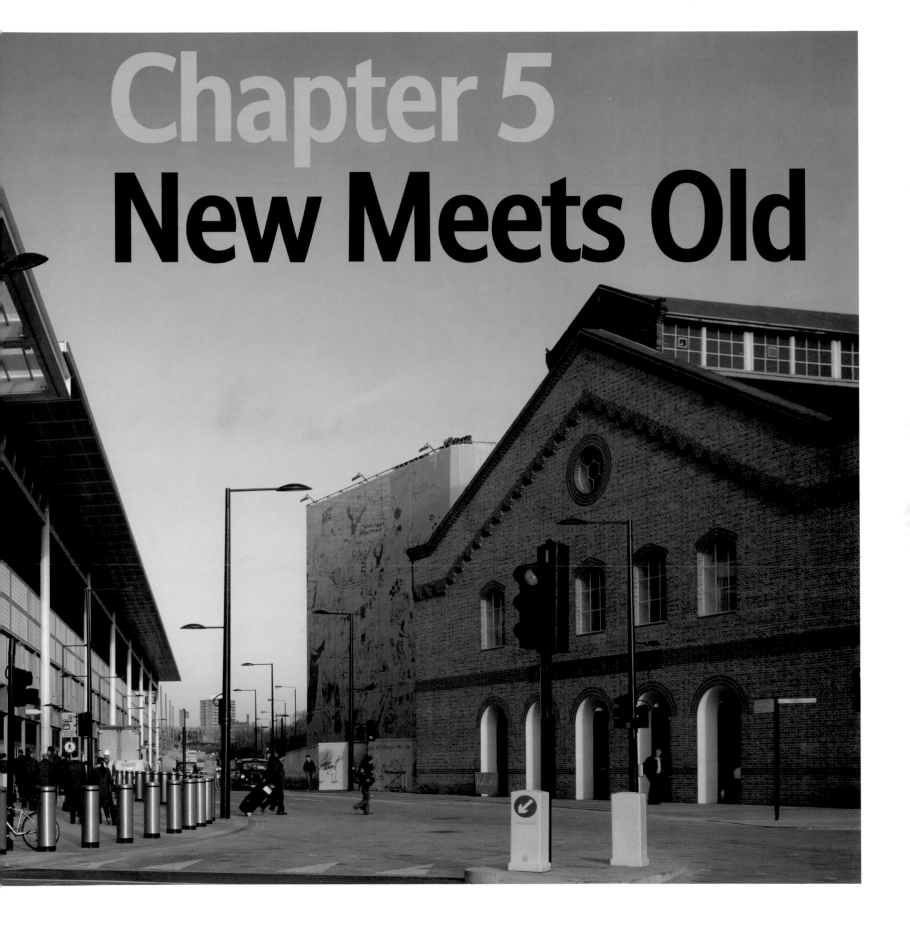

Chapter 5
New Meets Old

New Meets Old

Top: North gable and extension from platform level. **Above:** Junction between the north gable of the train shed and the new transition roof on the west side.

The Extended Station

The new St Pancras needed more and longer platforms, achievable only by extension and widening to the north. The importance of the original buildings raised a major stylistic question. There was never any particular symmetry between William Barlow's great arch and Sir George Gilbert Scott's Midland Grand Hotel – the combination worked by juxtaposition rather than by integration. Therefore, it was agreed that there should be no attempt at pastiche; the extension is a new and modern structure to the north of Barlow's train shed. Covering all 13 platforms, it is an aluminium-clad louvre-blade and glass roof, giving north light. Unlike the existing station, massive and heavy at street level, the extension has a lightweight canopy floating clear above the platform deck, so that passengers standing within the Barlow train shed don't feel 'shut in'.

The old and the new are separated by a great glass transept extending 22.5 metres (73 feet 9 inches) from the north gable to the extension roof, and more than 100 metres (328 feet) across. At each end are the new main entrances, also in glass to provide natural light deep into the station, down into the London Underground subway on the east side and for the descent to the new First Capital Connect platforms on the west. Passengers using this space can see above them the international trains and an end-on view of Barlow's north gable, and can look north to the new roof and through its glazing to the sky.

The platform deck of the station extension efficiently combines precast and *in situ* concrete, using the platform edges as the primary north–south beams. The ribbed soffits and lighting reflect the geometry of Barlow's undercroft to the south, to maintain the theme from the pedestrian concourses.

Looking south into the train shed from the extension.

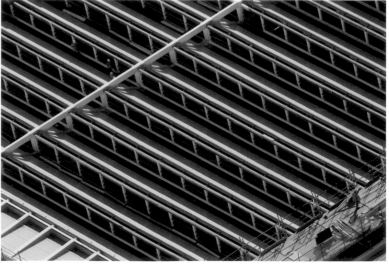

Aerial view of the St Pancras roof extension under construction.

Pages 80–81: The extended roof nestles between the original station and the façade of the German Gymnasium.

The New Roof

The new roof and façades to the extension of the Grade I listed St Pancras station have been developed in accordance with a number of design requirements, primarily to respect the setting and appearance of the existing Grade I listed train shed and the quality of the surrounding built environment.

The new roof is deliberately set away from the north end of the train shed to allow for the incorporation of a transitional zone that reflects the architectural cliché 'the best way to join something is to separate it'. The width of the transitional zone equates to the width of the central concourse at street level and also provides cover to the east and west domestic concourse areas at platform level. It signals 'the new heart of the station'.

The new roof and platform deck enclosure is designed as a contemporary structure contrasting with the architecture of the existing Barlow shed. Its

West entrance in Midland Road, looking north.

West entrance and transition roof in Midland Road.

East entrance looking south in Pancras Road.

Above: Erection of a column between transition and extension roofs, June 2003.

Below: The western side entrance.

slenderness assists in protecting significant local views of the Barlow train shed and Midland Grand Hotel from Midland Road and Pancras Road, and the important view north from the Barlow shed itself. Views from Hampstead Heath and Primrose Hill were also considered.

The design of the enclosing structure provides a substantial degree of shelter and weather protection for passengers travelling on both international and domestic services. Efficient and effective use is made of natural and artificial lighting by allowing natural light deep into the plan of the building at platform level, minimising the use of artificial lighting and reducing energy consumption. The internal and external appearance of the station after dark, when many commuters and passengers will arrive and pass through it, is also of particular importance. Effective artificial lighting not only enhances the profile of the building but is a positive benefit in increasing the perceived level of safety and security in the general area around the station.

The structure also provides natural ventilation, to minimise build-up of internal temperatures and enable fumes and pollution from trains to disperse at high level and ventilate out. In addition, sound energy generated within the station by trains is absorbed within the soffit.

The height of the underside of the roof plane was dictated by the level of the base of the end gable of the Barlow shed and the need to subordinate the new structure to the arched roof of the listed train shed.

The main extension roof canopy is supported on a series of 32 steel columns, in rows four abreast. They run the length of the platforms and are 21 metres (68 feet 10 inches) high. Three similar columns provide support to the southern edge of the transition roof, which lies between the Barlow shed and the main roof canopy. The outer east and west side columns pass in front of, and are tied back to, the platform deck edge, forming a colonnade in front of the concrete-clad column and external façade elements of the deck which march north of the station.

Glazing of the transition roof.

Taxi rank at the west entrance.

East side entrance leading to central concourse.

Ventilation gap and cantilevered brim on west wall of extension.

East Midlands train at the westernmost platform.

Transition roof meets the lower boom of the northern end screen. The design of the end arch ribs was probably inspiration for the Palais des Machines at the Exposition Universelle in Paris, 1889.

Far left, top and bottom: Northern gable end screen and transition roof.

Above: West side wall of extension at twilight and, **left**, detail.

Northern termination of the
extension roof from the east.

The louvres above the
central concourse.

Curved louvres inside the cantilevered
brim on the eastern side of the extension.

The Main Roof Canopy

The train deck is covered by a large canopy roof that extends the complete width of the deck. Its length shelters international trains entirely and substantially covers the domestic platforms. The roof structure comprises four trusses, approximately 2.6 metres (8 feet 6 inches) deep, running north to south, and slightly reduced depth trusses running east–west at 3.75 metre (12 foot 4 inch) centres.

A system of 'curved blades', consisting of curved steel rafters, is fixed within the structural depth of the roof trusses. Profiled metal sheeting forms the top of the blade while the underside is lined with curved perforated metal sheeting and backed with an acoustic lining. North-facing glazed openings through the main trusses allow the roof to ventilate naturally and enable diesel fumes to disperse into the open air.

A 4.5 metre (14 foot 9 inch) wide cantilevered brim runs around the edge of the east, west and north sides of the roof canopy and is located at the top level of the northernmost trusses. The east and west brims are supported by cantilevered steel beams extending from the top boom of east–west trusses at 3.75 metre (12 foot 4 inch) centres.

Cantilevered brim at twilight.

Cantilevered brim on the eastern side elevation.

Left: The transition roof treatment at the south end of the extension roof opposite the German Gymnasium.

Below left: The transition roof at platform level looking south towards original train shed.

Below right: The new roof meets the old on the eastern side of the station.

Above: The stepped levels of the transition roof against the extension roof. **Below:** The transition roof abuts the north-west tower.

The concept of the transition roof is to set the main deck extension roof canopy away from the Barlow train shed. Enclosing the central concourse, the transition roof runs the full width of the new station, at the junction with the Barlow train shed. A large void above the concourse on the east side provides emphasis to the main entrance to the new rail terminus. A smaller double-height void on the west side provides emphasis to the Midland Road entrance.

The transition roof main structure comprises steel beams suspended between the new main roof structure and the end screen of the Barlow train shed and supported on columns at the southern edge outside the confines of the shed. The main structural bridging beams of the transition roof are in line with the vertical stainless-steel ties introduced into the end screen. They are secured by a simple pin-jointed connection at each beam junction. The outer bay cantilevers, with an overhang of approximately 4.5 metres (14 feet 9 inches) extend as far as the outer edge of the main roof brim, but on a lower plane. The design expresses this separation with the transition roof being at a different level, and of a different form, to that of the main new roof extension.

The Façades

At street level, the east and west elevations comprise infill fenestration between the fair-faced concrete columns that support the deck extension. These infills consist of glazed flush panels and doors with louvred panels above. The roof columns form a colonnade in front of these façades.

The doors and glazed panels are approximately 2.6 metres (8 feet 6 inches) high, with a shadow gap against the louvred panels. Internal faces of Pancras Road bridge comprise terracotta-colour panelling facing the blockwork walls. These stand between fair-faced concrete columns and the painted metal grilles to openings between these panelled walls.

At platform level, a partial-height screen wall, approximately 5 metres (16 feet 6 inches) high from platform level and approximately 12.5 metres (41 feet) from street level, runs along the external faces of the new deck extension on both the east and west sides. The screens are not to the full height of the roof canopy or transition roof and do not touch the ends of the Barlow train shed. This physical separation of the structure provides further visual emphasis to the roof as an independent floating plane. On the west side of the station the screen walls extend the full length of the train deck and beyond to the adjacent embankment to shield adjacent properties, whereas on the east they extend to just beyond the main roof canopy, from where the spandrel panels continue up to just beyond the end of platform 13. North of the domestic concourse, the upper section comprises clear glass blocks supported in a stainless-steel framing. Below the glass blocks is a glass spandrel. The painted frame is connected to steel uprights fixed to the edge

Above: Detail of extension roof columns.
Below: Extension side screen detail.

beam of the concrete deck structure at 7.5 metre (24 foot 7 inch) centres and flush to the top of the screen edge. The lower edge of the glass spandrel steps upwards in a northerly direction to accord with the upward slope to the top of the concrete edge beam.

The opening between the top of the screen walls and the underside of the roof works with the system of roof blades to ensure sufficient and effective natural ventilation to clear the diesel exhaust from the trains. The height of the screens, together with the oversailing brim to the roof canopy, provides a balance between weather protection and ventilation to adjacent platforms.

Downlighting is housed between the lower edge of the glass spandrel and the concrete structure behind, set above a horizontal toughened glass soffit that is flush with the bottom of the glass spandrel. Uplighting has also been introduced within the top transom member of the screen.

Above: Extension roof and side wall ventilation gap.
Below: Eastern side of extension looking south.

The New Entrances

The eastern station entrance welcomes travellers from Pancras Road and the London Underground northern ticket hall into the domestic concourse. It is distinctly modern and functional, with the logotype 'St Pancras International', picked out in illuminated letters, appearing to levitate in the space between the roof and the lower entrance screen. The sign, visible from the Euston Road, changes in colour from white in the daytime to blue at night. The sliding entrance doors allow for large openings at ground level to maximise access and street activity, but enable the station to be fully secured when it is not in operation. A glazed canopy is also provided at the entrances to offer unobtrusive weather protection.

The interface with the subway from London Underground's new northern ticket hall presents itself as a circular glazed pavement light, penetrated by a slender steel column that soars dramatically upwards to support the clear glass of the transition roof. The circular feature is segmented by the glazed screen forming the entrance doors and resolves into the elongated shape of the subway entrance, appropriately forming a keyhole. The feature provides instant orientation of the two-level interface and forms a pool of natural light at the station end of the subway. A fully glazed balustrade with a stainless-steel handrail surrounds the glazed pavement light on a curved podium of black granite. On entering the station the traveller experiences the double-height volume of the entrance vestibule and wide concourse with the train

Above: Eastern entrance to central concourse.

Below: South-east corner of the station extension and the subway entrance to King's Cross northern ticket hall.

Western entrance to central concourse.

platforms above. Clear signage and logical layout speed travellers to their selected location, be that the ticket office, refreshments, shopping or platform. The transition roof exploits the transparency and lightness of the modern materials, especially the large panes of glass that allow light to permeate all levels from platform to concourse at street level. The different architectural languages bring together new and old or, dare we say, 'Neo-gothic meets Neo-classical' with all its new technologies, all of them complementing each other – and with a spatial panache that renders a new magical and joyful railway entrance to and exit from London.

The western entrance welcomes travellers from Midland Road with a wide and lofty portico in a modern style designed to contrast with the vibrant polychromatic Gothic architecture of the reconstructed west side and the sleek modern extension. The wide doorway leads into the domestic concourse with escalators down to the integral First Capital Connect station housed directly beneath the main station building. The ticket offices, train service information and shops that line the concourse are given a light and airy feel by the double-height glazed entrances. With the transition roof floating above, the architecture demonstrates how contemporary elements can enhance the old by relying on sensitive contrast rather than pastiche. The challenge was to relate the new to the old but at the same time create an extension and entrance that represent their own age with integrity. Here at the northern end of St Pancras, the historical building has been reinvigorated by a contemporary architectural intervention and thus provides a new civic space for London.

A new public entrance convenient for international travellers arriving by taxi on Pancras Road is positioned halfway along the 200 metre (656 foot) length of the restored east side buildings and is announced on to the external paving with a simple glazed cantilevered canopy, which hovers above the entrance with the words 'St Pancras International' illuminated on its edge. The four new openings that create this new entrance have been formed through four original arches that were at one time shop frontages. Each of the new doorways has been meticulously detailed with an additional prolapsed, polychromatic arch in red bricks and Ancaster stone. Taking their design from the original doorways, they are hung with new, solid oak double doors that match those previously used by draymen to gain access to and from the former beer warehouse in the undercroft beneath the station floor. The overall scale is monumental and a fitting 'gateway to Europe'.

Left: Eastern side of station, Eurostar main entrance on Pancras Road.

Facing page: Replica main door in oak, with wrought-iron window grilles and hinge straps for the Eurostar main street entrance on Pancras Road.

Chapter 6
Transformation

Transformation

Western side wall showing undercroft, platform level and arch ribs. The former booking hall is above the Eurostar ticket office and travel centre.

Unloading beer barrels from railway wagons in the undercroft, c.1960.

The Platform Deck and the Undercroft

For much of the station's life, the platform deck within the Barlow train shed and the undercroft have been two very distinct spaces. The platforms were bathed in the grandeur of Barlow's dramatic ironwork skeleton and Scott's exuberant polychromatic neo-Gothic masonry. Here the gentry dined in opulent refreshment rooms before boarding their Midland expresses. However, just feet below was the cavernous and windowless undercroft, unseen by the public unless they caught a glimpse into the darkness from one of the dray roads opening on to Pancras Road or Midland Road. The aroma from the open doors must have been maltily and yeastily pungent, as men toiled to unload barrels of ale from railway wagons in the gas-lit and claustrophobic gloom. Draymen loaded their horse-drawn drays here before setting off to the expectant public houses of London.

The undercroft resulted from the Midland Railway's decision to approach the Euston Road by running above the Regent's Canal. This placed the tracks some 5 metres (16 feet 6 inches) above street level and influenced the design of the train shed roof. Barlow's preliminary designs were for a roof of two or three spans. Since these would have required intermediate columns, this would have necessitated larger column sections in the undercroft with

commensurately larger foundations. Thankfully, Barlow decided upon a dramatic single-span arched roof of 73.15 metres (240 feet) span.

Construction was of cast-iron columns on a grid of 4.47 metres (14 feet 8 inches) supporting riveted wrought-iron girders. The distance between columns was the same as in brewery warehouses. Barlow wrote that, 'in point of fact, the length of a beer barrel became the unit of measure, upon which all the arrangements of this floor were based'.

On this grid of girders were riveted Mallet's patent rectangular wrought-iron 'buckle plates', which were dome-shaped plates with the centre rising some 76 millimetres (3 inches) high. These deck plates were overlaid with a layer of pitch and on top of this was laid the track. On the east and west sides of the undercroft the girders bore on substantial arched brick walls, which also formed the foundations for the train shed side walls above. The whole of this structure was set at a gradient of 1 in 336 throughout the length of the train shed, rising towards the north gable.

The most remarkable aspect of Barlow's design was the use of the framework of deck-supporting girders as the tie restraining the horizontal thrust from the arch roof. This dispensed with the need for bracing or buttressing at platform level and thus imparted an outstanding slenderness and elegance to the arched train shed structure. This device became known as Barlow's 'tie'.

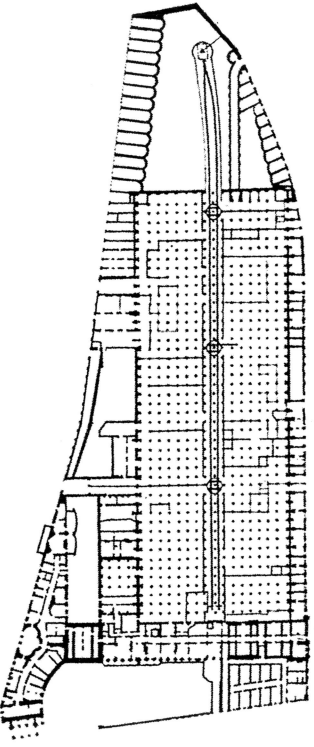

Plan of undercroft showing grid of columns and
the rail access with wagon-length turntables.

The beginning of the train shed erection, 1867, with the construction of the
first arch rib from the three-part mobile centring. It was designed to roll
along rails bolted to the buckle plate platform deck. The cross ties in the
platform deck are put in place to restrain the horizontal forces from the arch.

Top: Looking north-west, bomb damage to the platform deck penetrated through to the undercroft. **Above:** Looking north, repairs to the platform deck, 1942. St Pancras operated with three short platforms during the work. London, Midland & Scottish Railway engineers soon had the platform working again. Except for the glass, the famous single-span roof was undamaged.

Corrosion to the platform deck buckle plate.

The first structural change to the undercroft took place at the beginning of the twentieth century when the City and South London Railway (Northern Line City branch) was extended in 1907 from Moorgate to King's Cross and Euston. Two flights of stairs penetrated the buckle-plate structure and led down from the existing station concourse to a new pedestrian subway that was constructed at the south end of the undercroft to link with the new Underground station.

The second major change to the undercroft brought temporary and unexpected light into the gloom of the south-west corner. This was effected by the German air force on 10 March 1941 when a bomb dropped through the roof of the train shed. It penetrated the train deck and exploded in the undercroft, blowing a hole in the roof of the St Pancras branch tunnel of the Midland City line, more recently known as the First Capital Connect line, which passes under the station, and ripping apart a section of the wrought-iron deck.

As part of the hastily organised wartime repairs, 15 cast-iron columns were replaced with steel stanchions while another six were partially replaced by steel sections. Steel beams were installed at deck level to replace damaged wrought-ironwork and around 100 buckle plates were replaced by *in situ* concrete slabs.

Use of the undercroft for the storage of ale and other rail-related trades gradually declined, until it ceased in 1963. The undercroft was let to third-party tenants and the space was further subdivided.

Corrosion had long been a recurring problem in the deck structure. If there was one deficiency in Barlow's design, it was the lack of any drainage from the train deck. Despite the overall roof, driving rain was able to enter at the north end and trains that had just arrived through a rainstorm would drip water inside the train shed. The nature of the buckle plates with their raised crowns ensured that any such water drained to the low points above the rivets, from where it percolated through defects in the pitch on to the main structural girders. It was not until around 1901 that the Midland Railway installed a network of drainage channels suspended below the train deck with drainage pipes perforating the buckle plates. These perforations were necessarily above the lowest points of the buckle plates and so a modicum of water remained to continue the deterioration of the ironwork. The drainage system was only installed below the routes of the tracks, where access could be easily obtained for drilling. This did nothing to assist the situation beneath the vaulted brick platforms where water was free to percolate through from the track wells. In addition, the ends of girders built into the damp brickwork at the perimeter were prone to corrode.

Bringing Light into the Darkness

As part of the project, the most significant intervention made to the existing fabric of the train shed has been the opening up of four large light-wells in the platform deck. This has allowed the platforms and the undercroft to be seen as one connected space by visually uniting the two levels. The light-wells not only bring natural daylight into the otherwise dark undercroft but provide the location for lifts, stairs and escalators to allow passengers access to both levels.

Passengers arriving at street level and entering the north–south concourse, newly named The Arcade, can now experience a view of the station and its roof that was not previously available. At Arcade level they are also able to see arriving and departing Eurostar services within the Barlow train shed, which helps give clarity to the two levels and assists them in finding their way around and through the station. English Heritage deserves recognition for its decision to agree to this major alteration to the fabric of the station. Its normal requirements would have been 'minimal intervention' and 'totally reversible', which means only small alterations that can be returned to the original. English Heritage with the London Borough of Camden embraced these changes and saw opening the new vistas and creating a still greater sense of space as a positive development of the station.

So now, for the first time in 140 years, daylight floods into the once gloomy undercroft from the train shed above enabling it to be integrated as a key part of the passenger facilities of this international station. Passengers strolling through the retail arcade at undercroft level can gaze with wonder at the lofty heights of Barlow's train shed soaring above. This has been possible through the latest entrepreneurial vision and some very modern engineering ingenuity, building on the foresighted prowess of a great nineteenth-century engineer. London now has a new public space for the twenty-first century.

The interior of the car park in the vaults beneath St Pancras station, 1960–72. The platforms above were supported by the numerous cast-iron pillars.

Looking north from The Arcade through the platform deck slot to the train shed roof.

Looking south, daylight penetrating into The Arcade through the platform deck slot.

In a role reversal that would confuse a nineteenth-century passenger if he or she were to return to St Pancras, the intending international traveller enters the station at undercroft level through exact replicas of the original dray-road doors in the east side buildings. For where the beer-barrel storage used to be there are now wide concourses offering high-quality retail and leading to the international departure lounge. From there, travelators and lifts take passengers directly to their waiting trains in the Barlow train shed above.

No longer a dank and airless space, the undercroft is discreetly ventilated from an air plenum concealed beneath the floor, thus avoiding a plethora of overhead ducting obscuring the wrought-iron train deck. All this ironwork now remains visible with a 'loose fit' ceiling floating within the grid of iron girders.

Passengers arriving on international services walk along the platform to towards the station clock and descend to the undercroft. They leave the station through the west side buildings or head for a London Underground station, now reached directly from the south-west corner of the undercroft. Here a new corridor has been driven through the basement of the former Midland Grand Hotel to a new Underground ticket hall excavated beneath the hotel forecourt. Onward national rail connections are immediately available from St Pancras to services running on the Midland Main and First Capital Connect lines or high-speed services to Kent.

Top: Cast-iron column with capital and unused cleats.
Above: Eurostar departures hall lift shaft.

Eurostar departures lounge and travelator.

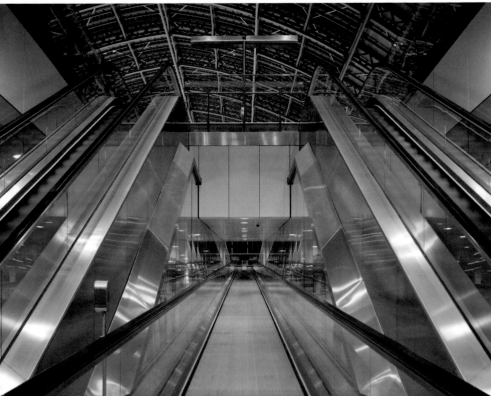

Top: Eurostar arrivals hall, side view of escalator.
Above: Eurostar departures lounge travelator glass screen.

Top: Intersecting travelators and escalators for arriving Eurostar passengers.
Above: Eurostar arrivals hall, brickwork end wall.

Repairs to the Platform Deck and Cutting the Barlow 'Tie'

Initial surveys undertaken for the Channel Tunnel Rail Link project showed that the occurrence of significant corrosion was relatively widespread. A number of bays were adjudged to be in need of replacement, while many others needed repair. It was essential that the deck structure accommodate all currently permitted railway vehicle loadings and have a two-hour fire resistance.

The stresses calculated under the required loading were found to be between 30 per cent to 85 per cent in excess of the design strength of wrought iron. These stresses were clearly unacceptable. Strengthening would be difficult to undertake on a riveted wrought-iron structure, especially one listed Grade I for architectural and historical importance.

It was therefore necessary that the existing wrought-iron deck structure be relieved of train loading by the installation a new 400 millimetre (15¾ inch) thick structural reinforced-concrete slab, cast above it but supported directly by the original cast-iron columns. These columns and their brick and stonework foundations were proven adequate to carry the new loads with some repairs and reinforcement.

Concreting the platform deck in bays.

Construction of platform deck supplementary slab beneath the northern gable end.

Undercroft under construction and opened to the platform deck, February 2006. Manoeuvring plant within the tight construction space was difficult.

Top: Removal of alternate tie girders at south end of train shed. **Above:** Completion of the tie removals and the casting of the platform deck edge detail.

The new reinforced-concrete deck now also carries the horizontal tie forces from the main roof arch, allowing the original tie structure to be relieved of load and the light-wells to be cut through the original framework of wrought-iron girders. Barlow's 'tie' has now been cut and replaced with modern materials. However, this allowed the retention of the historic wrought-iron deck structure while ensuring structural adequacy for the station into the future.

The cutting of the light-wells in the train deck had an additional benefit in terms of the repair of the undercroft structure. The cast-iron columns, wrought-iron girders and buckle plates displaced by the new platform-level openings provided original materials that were used to repair decayed and damaged ironwork in areas scheduled for retention. In this way, it was possible to reinstate the fabric lost at the south end by the installation of the 1907 subway, and to replace the steel and concrete repairs to bomb damage with original fabric material.

The train shed arch ribs spring from wrought-iron riveted plate boxes, known as 'boots', which themselves are founded on top of the undercroft's brick side walls. The tie girders from the train deck connect directly to the ends of these boots. Just as Barlow had given scant attention to the problem of water collecting above his iron train deck, here also there were deficiencies in detailing against water penetration and corrosion.

Especially vulnerable were the arches at the very north end of the train shed where driving rain could easily run down inside the hollow arches and collect within the boots. Furthermore, with the arches mostly built into the thick masonry walls dampness in the brickwork, especially from roof leakages during the station's many unloved and inadequately maintained years, had resulted in corrosion of the encased ironwork. In addition, on the west side of the station the outside ends of the boots stuck out of the base of the train shed walls and were encased only in damp earth fill and ash ballast from the railway sidings.

In order to introduce reinforced-concrete ties connecting to the new deck slab, it was necessary to cut back the brickwork at the base of the arches. This facilitated access to the 'riveter's hole' in the base of each arch. These holes had allowed a fitter to enter the box section in order to rivet the sections together. Now the holes were to form a convenient location to thread the new ties through the base of the arches. With the brickwork cut back, it was possible once again to enter the hollow arches through the original access hole and thus assess the degree of corrosion in each arch and its associated boot. Cores were cut in discreet locations to enable the present thickness and thus the degree of corrosion to be assessed. The sample discs were also tested so that the actual structural properties of the wrought iron were known. Detailed analyses, with assessments of corrosion losses and predictions of those expected in the future, were made to determine the degree of repair that was required to each boot.

Where corrosion was severe the structural components were carefully strengthened, while the bases of the arches at the north gable end required extensive renewal and reconstruction. The bases were encased in the two end towers and removal and reconstruction of brickwork was required to gain working access for the repairs. With the repairs to the train deck and arches complete, the station is again structurally sound with little evidence of the repairs and interventions. English Heritage and the project's heritage advisors ensured that the extensive and complicated repairs to the historic shed were safely completed without detracting from the appearance of the original. The train shed should serve for another century.

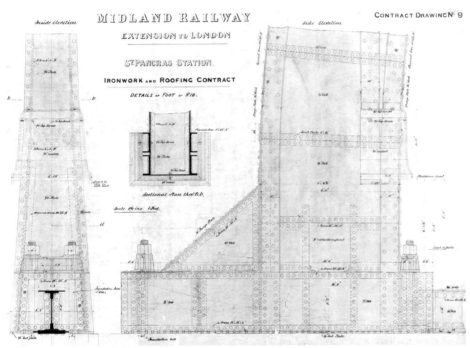

Contract drawing of the arch rib base, the cross tie retaining the horizontal forces from the arch.

Base of arch with sprags supporting the ornamental bell housing to the base of the rib.

Top: Inside the arch rib base through the riveter's hole.
Above: Exposed holding-down bolts on the inside of the arch rib base ready for restoration.

Eurostar Passenger Lounges

The international departures lounge is situated to the north-east of the refurbished undercroft and is located where the beer barrels used to be stored. The lounge is nonetheless an appealing and comfortable space that celebrates its history with exposed brickwork, wrought-iron girders and cast-iron columns. Unlike beer barrels, travellers demand an ambience with fresh air and lots of it. The design solution required the installation of underfloor ventilation – an air displacement system that has a series of air inlet grilles set in a domino pattern between the cast-iron column grid. This keeps the underside of the original girder and buckle-plate structure free of ductwork. All the ironwork is visible with a 'loose fit' ceiling, hovering within the ironwork grid, containing up and down lighting units, sprinklers and security cameras.

With such a grand building, Eurostar wanted to design a space that worked alongside its inherent features to define a unique experience that will become synonymous with this London landmark. Indeed, the richness of the Eurostar spaces, as with the rest of the station, often comes from the physical

Above and below: Eurostar departures lounge.

Eurostar platforms and lift.

constraints and lack of architectural freedom offered by a building of this kind. The result is an exceptional twenty-first-century space working in harmony with its elegant Victorian past.

Eurostar's interior design brief to Land Design Studios and Arup Associates was to transform the Victorian undercroft into a functional and inspiring space, capable of delivering seamless travel for millions of travellers each year. There was a conscious decision to design an experience as seen through the eyes of the traveller, not an interior.

The transition from the general station environment into the Eurostar areas is marked by the change in floor surfaces from terrazzo to jatoba, a sustainable hardwood. These wooden floors not only help to define the Eurostar spaces within the station but also add a touch of warmth and humanity to them.

Within the departure lounge there is a variety of seating, which has made full use of the space while allowing easy circulation and choice for travellers. The saddle-stitched leather on the formal seats combines comfort, quality and longevity. Angled benches weave between the Barlow columns to provide a contemporary contrast and more informal seating for families or friends to gather before departure.

The lounge is provided with multiple travelators, stairs and lifts up to platform level, delivering passengers to the centre portion of the Eurostar trains for boarding.

To maintain freshness and engagement within the lounge, and to bring the best of what London has to offer to travellers, Eurostar has worked with the National Gallery to bring travellers a virtual gallery of some of London's finest works of art. Over a hundred images can be viewed at one of the six installations within the terminal.

An 'Explore Europe' wall in the departures lounge allows travellers to discover their destinations before they travel, taking a virtual tour of cities and their streets or just checking out their hotel. An information zone removes the hassle from the simple things like buying tickets for the Paris Metro and can also help by recommending good restaurants and planning travellers' trips in more detail.

Above: Eurostar business lounge reception.
Below: Eurostar business lounge buffet bar.

Business Premier Lounge

Situated at platform level within the former east side buildings the Business Premier lounge is a magical space, mainly because of its volume. It has been designed to accommodate Business Premier travellers, both at street and platform level. In the early design stages it was agreed with English Heritage and the London Borough of Camden that it would be possible to take away an area of flooring at platform level. This had been installed in around 1910 following the dismantling of an existing pedestrian ramp that linked street level with the former arrivals side of the station at platform level. This area now has an exquisite helical staircase and glass lift which connect both undercroft (ground) and platform levels; the overall architecture plays similar tunes to the Sackler Gallery at the Royal Academy in Burlington House, where old and new complement each other.

The design of the lounge presented interesting challenges to the interior design team, but once again the constraints have created a unique space with a depth of character not achievable from a new build. The resulting combination of architectural features, furniture and technology creates a feeling of style and exclusivity.

The two floors are designed with different dwell times in mind. On the ground floor the immediate needs of the busy business traveller are met; he or she can pick up a paper and have a quick drink before boarding. The sleek helical staircase or lift takes them to platform level to a space geared towards a longer stay. Here they can relax, unwind, take refreshment, read a paper or make use of the office facilities before continuing their journey.

Eurostar business
lounge work area.

Longitudinal section of the booking hall, 1867, showing the roof truss supports, timber trussed members, lantern arcade and the king post supporting the roof covering, signed 'Geo. Gilbert Scott'.

The Two Booking Halls

The Midland Railway always had the convenience of its passengers foremost in mind and this is still the case with Eurostar and the new station. Barlow put considerable thought into his master plan for the original St Pancras, with departing and arriving traffic separated on the west and east sides respectively. Passengers arriving at the station by cab alighted on the west side immediately outside the booking hall, which itself was deliberately and conveniently adjacent to the departure platforms. Empty cabs had their own ramp back down to street level, from which they could make their way under the railway and re-enter the station through a discreet ramp at the north end, which took them directly to the arrivals platforms where they collected arriving passengers. A similar convenient circulation is today offered to arriving and departing Eurostar travellers, with a taxi set-down point on the east side in Pancras Road and a queueing point on the west side in Midland Road. Taxis are provided with a dedicated lane, helping to speed travellers to and from the station.

Scott's design for the booking hall did not disappoint the expectations of the Midland Railway directors for it was in the style of a medieval baronial hall with linenfold panelling and a lofty curved braced roof structure with a lantern light. Against the east wall, facing the arriving passengers, nestled the panelled ticket office. On the north wall, corbels supported blind Gothic arches, decorated with carvings of contemporary railway staff complete with a driver holding a carved stone locomotive.

The booking hall in its original form with the ticket office built against the western wall of the building, with the platforms to the left looking south. This view shows a truncated ticket office without its later clerestory windows, one of the downdraught furnaces and gas flare lighting.

The booking hall with the ticket office located on the western wall, 2001.

When the station opened on 1 October 1868 the booking hall was incomplete, and passengers bought tickets from a temporary office in the parcels station immediately to the north. At the same time, the Midland Railway had agreed additional expenditure on the provision of an iron, wood and glass roof outside the booking hall to protect arriving passengers alighting from their cabs. It is likely that this was completed by the time the booking hall opened in 1869.

Two enormous free-standing cast-iron downdraught coal stoves located in front of the west windows heated this voluminous space. Although some alterations were made to the internal ticket office itself, which involved removing the glazed clerestory, the booking hall remained largely untouched until later in the mid-twentieth century.

It narrowly escaped disaster during the First World War when, on the evening of 17 February 1917, a German R25 – a plane, not a Zeppelin – dropped five 50kg bombs on St Pancras hitting the tower and the carriageway. Eight people lost their lives and pieces of bomb can still be seen lodged in the brickwork above the carriageway.

Fortune smiled on the booking hall a second time in the Second World War, when a bomb hit the south-west corner of the train shed. However, it is likely that the resultant blast, which removed the glazing and roof coverings from the shed, also caused significant damage to the adjacent roof of the booking hall – the magnificent roof structure succumbed to the demolition hammer shortly afterwards and was replaced by a simple roof supported by Belfast roof trusses between 1980 and 1983.

Top: Booking hall ceiling and roof bracket supports, 1998.

Left: The departures covered way with the replacement glazed roof, 2001.

Restored columns and brickwork of
the former booking office doorway.

In 1980 the ticket office survived a different kind of attack when a British
Rail proposal to replace it with a modern 'travel centre' was defeated on
appeal at a public inquiry. As a compromise the original ticket office was
moved from the east wall to the west wall to suit the greater majority of
passengers, who now approached the booking hall from the tube staircases
in the station concourse rather than from the cab road. As part of this work,
two windows in the east wall were replaced by doorways to facilitate better
passenger flow.

Booking hall, 2001.

East side Eurostar main
entrance on Pancras Road.

Eurostar ticket office and travel centre under construction.

But now, 139 years after it opened, the booking hall has retired gracefully from its original function and will find a more relaxed use as a restaurant and bar. With international passengers arriving at the station at ground level rather than at platform level, the booking hall, too, has dropped down a level to the space immediately below.

For many years one of the secret spaces of St Pancras was in the vaults beneath the booking hall. Originally used for wine storage, and latterly as an electricity substation and boiler room, this once hidden space with its tall cast-iron columns and vaulted brick ceiling is now centre-stage as Eurostar's spectacular international ticket office. It is situated at the south-west corner of The Arcade and announces itself as part of this retail area's disciplined shopfronts, but once inside it the space is magical with its unexpected

Western arches under construction for the Eurostar travel centre.

Entrance colonnade to
Eurostar ticket hall.

volume. The flooring is again jatoba hardwood, which extends from The Arcade entrances through to the numerous ticket and information counters. The vaulted brick ceilings above the public areas are still visible, with a modern floating profiled aluminium ceiling below that supports the up and down lighting. There is a rich mixture of finishes with fair-faced walls set against highly polished panels which, behind the counters, form a backdrop, with mirror glazing extending to the brick vaulting. The illusion of additional space, almost into infinity, is delightful as well as mystifying.

Eurostar travel centre entrance.

Top and above: Eurostar travel centre and ticket hall entrance from The Arcade.

Rebuilt western façade, completed in 2006, and Midland
Grand Hotel departures gateway tower, completed in 1876.

21st-Century Gothic

21st-Century Gothic

It is not every day that a major part of a Grade I listed building is demolished while at the same time substantial alterations are made to much of the remainder. But then St Pancras International was not really first and foremost a conservation project. As a government-sponsored project, its prime function was to provide a convenient new London terminus for the Channel Tunnel train services in the underused structures of St Pancras station. The government facilitated the restoration project by using the Channel Tunnel Rail Link Act to disapply the Planning (Listed Buildings and Conservation Areas) Act 1990. But all was not lost for conservationists as the CTRL Act set out certain minimum repair works that would be required to the fabric, and further stipulated that London & Continental Railways were to enter into a deed of agreement with English Heritage and the London Borough of Camden to ensure that the resultant works of alteration and repair were carried out in a sensitive manner appropriate to the Grade I listing of the building.

Inevitably, over the 135 years since its creation, many unsympathetic alterations had been made to the station. As the nineteenth-century euphoria over the designs of Sir George Gilbert Scott and William Henry Barlow waned,

Above: West side former goods depot viewed from the rear of the hotel building showing the departures carriage way route back to Midland Road.

Above: Western side wall with glazing strip in train shed roof.

Right: West side former goods depot from the north-west tower looking south towards the hotel building and Euston Road.

Western side walls in the former goods depot without any roofing.

the Gothic grandeur of St Pancras had become something of a millstone around the necks of the Midland Railway and its successors. With changing patterns of traffic and the developing needs of the railway, alterations began to be made in expedient ways. Money for repairs was often in short supply and water ingress began to take its toll, while the repairs that were made did not always use sympathetic or even matching materials. Sometimes, when money was available, it had not been spent wisely and original delicate fabric was damaged. This had been earlier demonstrated by the aggressive cleaning of the brickwork and stonework of the train shed walls, using harsh abrasives and rotary sanding discs.

When the conservation teams moved into the station as the last trains for the East Midlands left the old buildings in 2004 there was much to be done to restore the dignity of Scott's extravagant neo-Gothic realisation. Works to restore the masonry fabric centred around four areas: the train shed walls (of which the north elevation of the former Midland Grand Hotel formed part); the east side buildings fronting on to Pancras Road; the west side buildings on Midland Road; and the masonry structures of the undercroft beneath the train shed.

Far left: Concrete lintels inserted into doorway openings replacing brick arches between the kneeler stones that were fortunately retained.

Left: The Shires Bar doorway defaced with insertion of an inappropriate frame.

Herringbone spandrel.

The Principles of Conservation

The station foundations and masonry were built as part of Waring Brothers' 1865 contract with the Midland Railway Company. The specification of this contract survives in the National Archives at Kew. However, it is clear from the minute books of the Bedford–London Extension Committee 1864–1868–1872 that variations were made during construction, partly due to fluctuations in brick supply and contract delays but also to reduce the contract cost.

The Midland Grand Hotel was built under subsequent contracts overseen by Scott, for which the minute books provide an intermittent account of materials used to complement Scott's drawings.

Brickwork

The specification for Waring's initial contract describes the materials to be used. The bricks generally were:

> to be well burnt sound hard square and neatly formed, uniform and size of a quality equal to the best Cowley stocks. The face bricks must be picked of uniform colour and precisely equal dimensions to the bricks used in the interior of the work so as to secure a good bond and neat joints and all the face bricks must be laid alternately headers and stretchers. No bricks are to be used warm from the kiln and when required they shall be wetted or soaked in water. The whole of the

Exemplar of west side façade panel.

Top and above: East side buildings upper storey, exterior brickwork in poor repair and ineffective rainwater downpipes. Train shed interior west wall with Minton tiling frieze showing signs of water penetration.

joints are to be flushed up solid with mortar and grout in every course, in no course are the joints to exceed ¼ inch [6.3 mm] in thickness and all brickwork is to be carried on and completed in every respect to the satisfaction of the Engineer.

The eventual choice of facing bricks and their suppliers is documented to some extent in the minute books. A favourable quotation from Gray of Swannington in Leicestershire was subsequently withdrawn and the supply contract was placed with Edward Gripper's Nottingham Patent Brick Company. His company produced machine-made bricks of consistent quality on a large scale, fired in Hoffman kilns. With the project requiring some 60 million bricks, a shortage of bricks became a problem at various times during construction and further supplies came from Tucker and Sons of Loughborough in Leicestershire. The soft red, rubbing bricks used in the arches and quoins were supplied by a number of brickyards including Wheeler Brothers of Reading, Allen of Ballingdon and Lawrence of Bracknell. Ultimately, therefore, a variety of bricks was used throughout the station.

Minton tiling frieze in cleaned condition after minimal treatment.

Pancras Road shopfronts required extensive work to
remove paint and to recreate the mortar pointing.

Cleaning of trial brickwork
panel on eastern façade.

North-west tower in poor condition with
missing stone frieze and cappings.

Dray doorcase and arch
in poor condition.

Restoration of window cases and stone plinths on the west side of the train shed.

Above: Eastern façade restoration including the replacement of window and door frames.

Right: English bond in use on the blind panels of the western façade showing a course of stretchers and headers and the use of snap headers.

Brick bonding was to be English throughout (alternate courses of headers and stretchers). Arch rings were to be properly bonded and not laid in successive unbonded half brick rings. This was more troublesome for the bricklayer, but produces a stronger arch. Hoop iron of 25.4 by 1.6 millimetres (1 inch by $\frac{1}{16}$ inch) section was to be built into every fourth course of arches at 229 millimetres (9 inch) spacing, for the declared purpose of 'more effectively tying the work together' although it is likely that this was not done as no evidence of it has been found during the execution of the repairs. Joints of arches and face work were 'to be raked out and tuck pointed with white mortar in a careful and workmanlike manner where ordered and to the reasonable satisfaction of the engineer'.

Western side wall restoration of doorcase stone plinths and millstone grit ashlar courses.

Mortar for both brickwork and stonework was to be made from 'well and freshly burnt lime of approved quality from the best beds of Barrow-upon-Soar Lias limestone, properly and carefully slaked and covered for 8 hours at least then mixed with clean sharp sand 2:1 sand:unslaked lime.' The least possible quantity of water was to be used. Mortar was to be thoroughly well ground. The Lias limestone of Barrow in Leicestershire yielded a natural eminently hydraulic lime more akin to natural cement, which accordingly set partly by reaction when mixed with water and subsequently through the carbonation of the lime.

Grout was to be made from tempered mortar with the necessary quantity of water. Concrete, to be used in foundations and where elsewhere described on the drawings, was to comprise clean gravel and sand with fresh burnt hydraulic lime from Barrow, in the proportions of six parts of gravel, sand and best ballast to one part of lime. Thus 'concrete' was to be made with lime, and not, as is nowadays the practice, with Portland cement.

Stonework

Barlow's specification for Waring's contract calls for stone in foundations to be Bramley Fall or Derbyshire gritstone of uniform textures. Bramley Fall is strong, durable, but coarse-textured millstone grit sandstone. Derbyshire gritstone is similar.

Scott specified the use of Ketton and Ancaster, both oolitic limestones, and Mansfield Red for interior and exterior elevations. Mansfield White was used for stairs and steps. The Mansfield stones are Dolomitic sandstones, with substantial content of both calcium and magnesium carbonate.

Additional decorative stones including granites from Shap and Peterhead were specified by Scott for his more exuberant work in the Midland Grand Hotel.

Corsehill quarry.

Glebe quarry.

Above and below: East side shops, merchandise
spilling on to the pavement, 2001.

The Strategy for Masonry Repairs

The Minimum Environmental Requirements, which formed part of the development agreement between the Secretary of State and London & Continental Railways, set out certain requirements to repair, restore and refurbish the train shed interior walls and the east side buildings' elevation on to Pancras Road. In respect of the latter, the requirements for the ground-floor shop frontages were more prescriptive as they sought to return the overall appearance to as near the original as possible.

Agreement was reached with English Heritage and the London Borough of Camden that repair work to the retained fabric would follow the approach set out in the English Heritage publication *Repair of Historic Buildings: Advice on Principles and Methods*. This publication defines the primary purpose of repair as being 'to restrain the process of decay without damaging the character of buildings or monuments, altering the features which give them their historic or architectural importance, or unnecessarily disturbing or destroying historic fabric'.

It was agreed that repairs and cleaning were required to ensure structural adequacy and stability, weather protection, durability and acceptable appearance.

Dray doorway on Pancras Road with expedient flue.

Eastern façade dereliction.

Acceptable appearance is important as it influences the perception of both the original architectural design and the quality of the building function. Cleaning contributes to improvement in both respects, although it must be tempered by the need to minimise the risk of damage to the fabric during the cleaning process. Discreetly executed, minor repairs contributed to improving appearance, as in the repair of the very numerous screw holes from former billboards inside the train shed.

The three 'bilities' are well known in conservation circles where reversibility, breathability and flexibility are the rules. To these we found we had to add vulnerability. The adaptation, alteration and conservation of sensitive historic buildings is fine in theory but in execution it is not dissimilar to holding a Rugby Union international in a museum of Venetian glass. While conservators attended to the delicate needs of fragile historic materials, heavy construction plant was manoeuvring within the interior spaces excavating, dismantling and re-erecting.

Western side wall with ferns below tiled frieze.

Repairing the Train Shed Interior

Understandably, the train shed interior had borne the brunt of 135 years of railway operation. Some original door and window openings had been bricked up while others had been crudely enlarged to facilitate access by electric trolleys and barrows or, in the case of the refreshment rooms at the south end, to suit changing needs and fashions. As a result, original decorative stonework and cast-iron windows had been removed or damaged while retail units had been constructed against original brickwork. Furthermore, the history of the development of building services and sanitary engineering from the nineteenth to the twenty-first century could be intimately traced through the plethora of cabling and pipework running across, or rudely cutting through, ornately moulded brickwork and stonework.

Added to this was the damage caused by years of water penetration. If there was a weakness in Barlow and Scott's original design, it was to be found in the design and location of the parapet gutters to the train shed which sat atop the shed side walls. These were basic lead troughs on timber bearers, and any blockages or leakages resulted in the water overflowing on to the top of the masonry and then flowing down the interior wall surface. As a result there were some quite magnificent examples of buddleias and ferns growing from the mortar joints before repairs were commenced.

All this water caused serious damage both in staining and salt exfoliation of the masonry surfaces and the risk of frost damage. Thankfully, the brickwork was found to be sound although badly stained in many areas and refacing, which would have been damaging to the archaeology of the fabric, was not required.

Manoeuvring plant and materials within the tight construction space was difficult, February 2006.

West side wall of train shed has 15
new openings created for retail units.

Detail of door head for new openings in
western side wall of the train shed.

Pancras Road unrestored façade
from Euston Road, 2001.

Restoration Works at Platform Level

The west wall of the station at platform level has also been altered; the existing
arrangement had a rich assortment of openings ranging from those in the
existing former booking hall to more modest door and window openings fronting
the then public concourse. Further north, the tracks for the original platform 1
ran adjacent to the wall, which was decorated with blind arches. With agreement
from English Heritage and the London Borough of Camden a total of 15 new
openings have been created through the blind brickwork arches, giving access
from the new extended public concourse area into new station retail facilities.
These openings take their detailing from the east of the station and although the
detailing is simplified they are rich in scale and modelling. Their heavily detailed
doors and associated ironmongery give the retail units dignity and taste.

Repairing the East Side Buildings

The east side buildings form the eastern elevation on to Pancras Road. As
originally conceived, there were coal offices in the neo-Gothic arched vaults at
street level, and station offices and waiting rooms at platform level above were
reached through openings in the train shed east wall. In the middle was a dog-leg
ramp leading from platform level down to the street as an egress for excursion
passengers arriving on platform 7 on the east side of the train shed. The whole of
this ensemble was punctuated at street level by a series of dray roads, accessed
through huge timber doors, and leading to the beer stores in the undercroft.

At the south end, a pedestrian route was created in 1907 at ground level,
between the south end of the station from platform level through the east side

Pancras Road façade after restoration
and cleaning, February 2008.

East side façade and north-east tower restoration complete showing flashings and lower slated roof.

buildings and down to the King's Cross St Pancras Underground station. This subway was removed as part of the Channel Tunnel Rail Link works and the affected rooms have been returned to conventional use.

Apart from the structural alterations that were undertaken during the early history of the building, little maintenance seems to have been carried out to the elevation. The ground storey was cleaned in the 1970s, but the upper storey still retained 135 years of soot and grime when works commenced.

To prepare the building for its new functions as an international station, much of the interior was gutted, removing the later accretions and inserted upper floors. A new upper floor was constructed and the original roof and trusses were removed to enable the loft space to be used uncluttered by structural elements for a new plant room, for which ventilation intake louvres were inserted at eaves level behind the parapet. Chimneys were demolished and rebuilt as ventilation exhausts. A new steel roof structure was clad with Ffestiniog slate, matching the train shed roof behind.

The brickwork and stonework to the Pancras Road façade wall was fully cleaned for the first time in the building's history and decayed stonework and brickwork were carefully repaired.

At the north end of the east flank wall, the north-east stair tower had been exposed below platform level by the demolition of the northern vaults and was refaced to match the original adjacent work.

In the centre of the elevation, the new four-arch entrance to the station was constructed with heavy oak doors to replicate the original dray road openings.

The chimney stacks viewed against the train shed during renovation, August 2005.

Undercroft repairs to areas damaged by
Second World War bombing, April 2005.

Repairing the Undercroft

The masonry structures of the undercroft were much akin to railway viaducts, being continuous arched structures on the east and west sides. To the south, the undercroft was bounded by the north basement wall of the former Midland Grand Hotel. To the north, the old retaining wall was demolished to provide a link through to the new station extension.

The side walls were constructed of dark multicoloured stock bricks in lime mortar with half-inch joints. There was none of the finesse of George Gilbert Scott's brickwork above, for this was functional engineering work to support the massive loads of the train shed. It is likely that some or all of these bricks were fired on site as contemporary photographic evidence shows brick-making at St Pancras.

Not only was this brickwork functional, it was also within a busy working area of the station where it was subject to everyday knocks and scrapes from the loading and unloading of wagons. The Second World War bomb had caused damage in the south-west corner by lifting the ironwork to the train deck and fracturing the brickwork at the perimeter. All of the damaged brickwork was cut out and sensitively repaired using salvaged bricks and the undercroft was then cleaned to remove 135 years of dirt and grime. The majority of the arches on the west side were originally built with blind infills and these were opened out to allow access through the arches to the rebuilt west side of the station.

One of the three brick moulding machines
on the site of St Pancras station, 1866–67.

Damage to brick and stone
voussoirs in the dray doorcases.

Midland Road view of the rear of the hotel and covered
way together with the undercroft throughway entrance.

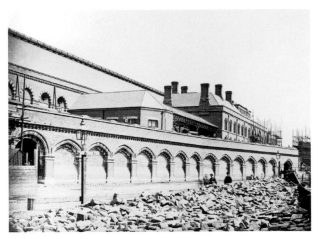

West side buildings in 1867, including Barlow House and the booking office and retaining wall against Skinner Street (now Midland Road) before the erection of the Midland Grand Hotel.

Rebuilding the West Side

The major piece of reconstruction work was centred on the west side of the station in Midland Road. Here, west of the train shed and north of the booking hall, the Midland Railway had laid out coal drops and a parcels station as part of their original concept. Constructed partly on a brick viaduct and partly on retained fill, the west side was mostly open to the weather and water penetration had caused major damage to the fabric. There was evidence that the elevation to Midland Road had been repaired and rebuilt several times in its lifetime. An inscribed brick identified major repairs undertaken between 1932 and 1935.

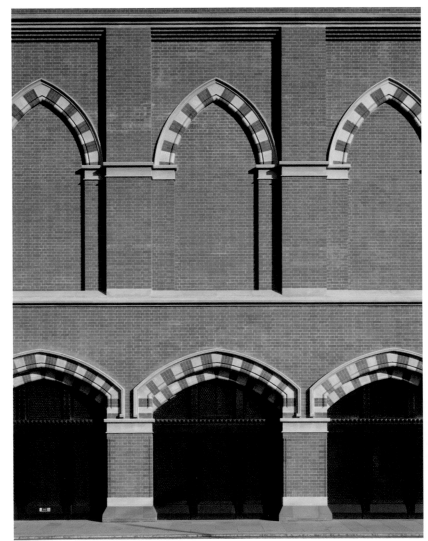

Above and right: Western elevation with blind arches and grilles for machine rooms on the lower storey.

A Midland Railway horse-drawn wagon, carrying milk and sundry goods, at the north end of platform 6, c.1912.

As originally constructed by the Midland Railway, the parcels station immediately abutted the north wall of the west side buildings, now known as Barlow House, and was fronted by an iron and glass canopy to shelter the horse-drawn wagons. To the north were the railway sidings running down the western side of the train shed. On the west side, a cobbled cab road dropped down from the glazed cab rank alongside the booking hall, emerging through a brick archway to join Midland Road. Alongside the foot of the cab road, a spiral staircase descended to the Metropolitan branch tunnel (now used by Thameslink trains) where a signal box was located in the smoky gloom.

The original elevation to the west side was formed of a series of Gothic arches, blind when fronting filled areas and mostly fitted with doors when opening on to arches. At the south end, an east–west dray road gave access

Western façade from Midland Road.

Above and below: Western façade from Midland Road.

to the undercroft. To the north, an arched canopy protected the railway sidings and an ornate multi-arched parapet wall screened the trains from direct view.

In 1892, the Midland Railway revamped much of this area and constructed a much larger roofed area for the delivery of goods, which resulted in the construction of a high screen wall along much of the upper level of the Midland Road elevation.

But there was another issue altogether at play here; the Midland Railway's Metropolitan branch (now known as the First Capital Connect line) runs in a tunnel under the west side of the station before curving sharply to head east. The need to construct a new cut-and-cover subsurface station on the tunnel alignment beneath Midland Road and closely adjacent to the international station's foundations, together with the poor condition of the west side buildings, signed the demolition warrant for this part of the station.

Departures carriage way covered roof.

Western side building
from Midland Road.

English Heritage was of the view that any reconstruction of this original elevation must emulate Scott's original designs and so the new building was designed as what must surely be a unique example of twenty-first-century Gothic.

The new west side wall follows the original building line on Midland Road, although the accommodation was designed specifically to provide facilities that are relevant to the operation of the new international station. At the north end, the new building houses mechanical plant on three levels, servicing the international station, and conceals the ventilation shaft from the new First Capital Connect station beneath. In the middle of the flank wall at ground level is the taxi pick-up area for the main station together with the escape stair from the First Capital Connect station below, while at the south end a delivery

Western façade detail
of plant room doors.

Midland Metropolitan branch connection tunnel opened out for the building of the station for First Capital Connect services. The new construction, left, the original brick-lined tunnels, right, November 2004.

Western façade looking towards the blind arches of the top storey.

bay services both main station and hotel. At platform level, there is new retail accommodation opening out on to the west side concourse. Above platform level, the design provides a podium for the new hotel extension.

There were significant physical constraints affecting the new design. In addition to the First Capital Connect line tunnel, London Underground's Northern and Piccadilly line tunnels run under the southern half of the site, substantially restricting locations for piled foundations in this area. The structure of the new building is of steel framing with precast concrete floors, the foundation constraints resulting in long clear spans because of the limited points of support. Abutting the train shed, the structure is nevertheless independent and neither provides support for nor takes support from the original building.

Western façade stone and brickwork arches.

Western train shed side wall new openings.

Reconstructed western façade looking towards the rear of the hotel building.

The new brick and stone façade to Midland Road was designed as a traditional loadbearing masonry structure and is only tied back to the steelwork frame for wind-loading resistance. Constructed with lime mortar based on the original nineteenth-century specification, it has no intermediate expansion joints. Concealed movement joints were provided at the three abutments with the existing fabric to allow for any movement in the new foundations.

At street level, the elevation is a near-identical replica of the original Midland Road façade. Above, it makes reference to the design of the 1892 screen wall while responding to the ornate masonry, designed by Scott, of the train shed west wall and tower and the former Midland Grand Hotel to the south. Detailing and moulding profiles for the rubbed brickwork and stonework were taken from the original mouldings or, where these were not appropriate, from a scholarly study of moulding profiles in use elsewhere on the station and former hotel.

As would be expected, variations were found between original mouldings on the same façade due to the nature of hand-working the stone. There has also been loss of original profile in many instances due to weathering. The new profiles have, where necessary, been standardised to accord with the sharpest and most consistent details found.

The openings in the new elevation reflect the new station facilities located behind and are variously filled with contemporary glass doors for taxi access and the Thameslink emergency escape stairway, and with painted cast-aluminium screens that conceal the mechanical and electrical plant rooms and service areas. The entrance to the deliveries bay at the south end is formed from a steel lintel supported on the adjacent brick piers. The face of the lintel has been finished with ornate cast-iron panels salvaged from the 1892 entrance to the Somers Town goods depot that had been on the west side of Midland Road.

Cantilevered canopies formed of a single sheet of toughened clear glass extending over the width of each opening provide shelter at the taxi pick-up zone. The northern mechanical plant area at platform level has recessed blind Gothic panels between piers as windows are not appropriate there. The arches on this section of the façade are taller, reflecting the increased height of the plant area, with its open enclosure behind the roof-level parapet effectively forming a third storey.

At platform level, there are passenger and retail facilities with access from the Barlow train shed through the 15 new openings in the shed west wall; these are framed in brick and stone in the style of original openings elsewhere in the station.

Although effectively a new structure, the rebuilt west side buildings form a northern continuation of the Midland Road western elevation of the former Midland Grand Hotel and abut the north-western tower of the train shed. It is thus seen against the original nineteenth-century workmanship with which it can be closely compared.

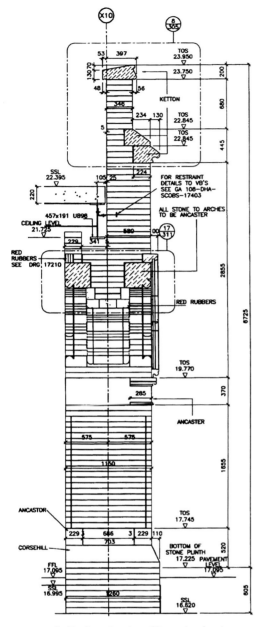

Section through arches of the western façade.

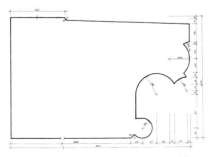

Detailed drawing for replacement stone moulding.

At the Brick Development Association Brick Awards 2006, the reconstruction of the west side buildings received the Supreme Winner and Best Craftsmanship awards, and the brickwork contractor, Irvine Whitlock, was named 'Specialist Brickwork Contractor of the Year'.

In making the award the judges said, 'Once in a while you get a project where the quality of work is simply so good that it rises above anything seen before. This is certainly the case with the rebuilt western elevation at St Pancras, the finest evocation of brickwork ever seen.'

Procuring New Bricks for St Pancras

After 135 years of progress in the brick industry finding replacement bricks was not going to be an easy task. The original bricks for St Pancras had been supplied by Edward Gripper's Nottingham Patent Brick Company with additional bricks from Tuckers of Loughborough, both sited on a Keuper marl clay seam. These bricks had been manufactured by a patent process which produced a very precise smooth brick. Neither the bricks nor their patent processes are now available. Furthermore, the majority of the original brickwork had been heavily cleaned, with the result that the original smooth fireskin had been lost. The decision was therefore taken to attempt to match the original brickwork in its condition as found, rather than as it was when new.

Charnwood Forest Brick, who fortuitously were not far from the now defunct Tuckers works near Loughborough, was the only company able to offer a brick in clay that was similar to the original. To do so they had first to develop a refined handmade process specifically for St Pancras. To achieve the quantities of 12,000 to 15,000 bricks a week, six skilled brick-makers were employed to create these special bricks by hand.

New red rubbing bricks for the gauged brick arches and other decorative brickwork were supplied by the Bulmer Brick and Tile Company, whose brickyard is just a few miles from the now defunct Allen works in Ballingdon, Suffolk, which supplied some of the original rubbers.

Chapter 8
London's Best-Connected Station

London's Best-Connected Station

New and upgraded passenger connections to the existing underground railways at King's Cross St Pancras, together with a new station for First Capital Connect main line services, are essential to the success of St Pancras International in catering for the increase in passengers arriving and departing from the new terminus.

King's Cross St Pancras is one of the busiest stations on the London Underground system serving 65,000 passengers in the morning peak. Six Underground lines come together here: the Hammersmith & City, Circle, Metropolitan, Northern, Piccadilly and Victoria lines. The station also provides a direct passenger interchange with St Pancras and King's Cross main line stations.

It was agreed that the redevelopment of King's Cross St Pancras Underground station should include works to improve passenger circulation and relieve congestion. The improvements would provide step-free access from street level to platforms for the benefit of passengers with impaired mobility, and develop the station management's command and control facilities to be commensurate with the size of the new station.

St Pancras and King's Cross joined below ground with the London Underground lines through three ticket halls – two new and one enlarged to deal with the additional passengers.

Exploded montage of the western ticket hall, Circle and Metropolitan lines and Euston Road.

Western ticket hall cross section, looking west.

Page 142: London Underground poster, 1980s, making sure people using the newly electrified St Pancras to Bedford suburban services knew they would be able travel onwards to other London destinations by five, now six, Underground services. The line added since the 1980s is the Hammersmith & City.

London Underground Ticket Halls

By 2011, four years after the opening of the Channel Tunnel Rail Link, it is predicted that some 92,000 passengers will be using the Underground station in the morning peak. Accordingly, major improvements have been made to the London Underground entrances and platform subways; the final stage of these works will be complete by 2010. There are three main elements to these works: an enlarged and refurbished Tube ticket hall to upgrade the original one located at the front of, and beneath the forecourt of, King's Cross main line station; a new ticket hall and passenger entrance/exit for the Hammersmith & City, Circle and Metropolitan lines, known as the western ticket hall, located beneath the forecourt of the former Midland Grand Hotel fronting St Pancras on the Euston Road; plus a major new passenger facility and ticket office with direct connections to the deep tubes of the Northern, Piccadilly and Victoria lines, north of the former Great Northern Hotel, between King's Cross and St Pancras stations, known as the northern ticket hall.

The Original London Underground Tube Ticket Hall

The circulation space within the original Tube ticket hall, now much upgraded, has been enlarged, giving overall clarity to the layout. The ticket office and ticket machines have been located in the back wall of the circulation area and in front of new accommodation for station staff. This main circulation area is united by a semicircle of staircases that allows views down into the newly organised ticket gate line. Lifts are also available to all levels of the ticket hall. A new subway under the Euston Road allows the original subway to be subsumed within the circulation space, providing seamless interchange between the deep-level Tube lines and the Metropolitan and Circle lines. A resited station operation room equipped with the latest control systems has picture windows to give the operator a clear view of the circulation areas and the travelling public a sense of security. A further safety feature, not apparent to the public, is a dedicated emergency response lift to the deepest part of the station.

Western ticket hall excavation of former hotel forecourt, looking north.

The enlarged Tube ticket hall.

Western ticket hall looking east towards the Tube ticket hall.

South wall of the former hotel below street level, the entrance to St Pancras International station, left.

The London Underground Western Ticket Hall

The newly built western ticket hall opened its doors to the public on Sunday 28 May 2006, and takes its general layout and three-dimensional appeal from all the qualities of space and volume found within St Pancras. London Underground assumed responsibility for the design and construction, independently from the works at St Pancras station. Arup, under the direction of London Underground together with architects Allies and Morrison, developed the design to improve operability and to integrate it with the London Underground congestion relief proposals. With project management from Metronet Rail, London Underground has delivered an open and pleasing facility.

The space for this new ticket hall has been created by excavating the forecourt of the former Midland Grand Hotel, extending and deepening the original basement area into a spacious two-storey galleried enclosure. Access is provided from Euston Road to the south and Pancras Road to the east with subways connecting the western ticket hall to the main Tube ticket hall. Step-free access is provided from street level to platforms along a ramp, and lifts are located along the main passenger circulation routes. The construction work was difficult and complicated, as it involved working close to the operating Underground railway and the busy Euston Road, while protecting the fabric of the Grade I listed former hotel immediately above it.

The internal northern façade wall is the original hotel basement and foundation wall. This has now been faced with bricks made from the same source of clay as the original hotel façade bricks, which anchor the internal fit-out of the ticket hall to St Pancras. The overall effect – that St Pancras seems to grow out of the western ticket hall – is further amplified by replacing the original forecourt light-wells along the elevation of the hotel's façade. Signage apart, travellers know they have arrived at St Pancras by the warmth of this new brickwork.

Space beneath the former hotel
building looking towards The Arcade.

The creation of a new entrance from London Underground's western ticket hall beneath the former hotel and into the St Pancras International undercroft concourse is thrilling. Passengers emerge from the Underground with its constraining passageways into the bright and spacious western ticket hall, before passing through to St Pancras International and experiencing, for the first time, the soaring space and grandeur of Barlow train shed.

This is a grand entrance, announced by four brick-faced, polychromatic arches that have been created from four of the basement window openings in the former hotel, which now beckon the traveller into the international station beyond. These openings are surmounted with flat steel lintels fitted with round-headed bolts to simulate original riveted wrought-ironwork. It is the attention to detail that makes the space appear as if it had been created by either Barlow or Scott.

Western ticket hall entrance into
St Pancras station through the
polychromatic brickwork arches.

Space beneath the former hotel where the western ticket hall entrance to the station has since been constructed, February 2006.

Undercroft to be opened out into an entrance for passengers coming into St Pancras from the western ticket hall.

Existing doorway to be opened out into the western ticket hall entrance to St Pancras station.

The construction of this new entrance required some heroic engineering, cutting through the basement and foundations of the hotel building above. Significant loads had to be carried by new structural steel members down to concrete foundations that have been stitched into the original fabric. New Charnwood brickwork on the newly faced arches and doorways is revealed as passengers enter the station from the newly constructed London Underground western ticket hall. Six steel columns together with beams carry the enormous loads from above. Extensive underpinning has been cleverly disguised with new lime-plastered vaults, which are profiled to match the existing brick vaults.

Space beneath the former hotel supported by cast-iron columns looking towards the London Underground western ticket hall.

Simulation of the London Underground
northern ticket hall after enlargement.

The London Underground Northern Ticket Hall

A new northern ticket hall planned to open in 2010 is located on the western flank of King's Cross, opposite the new main entrance to St Pancras. It has a direct link into St Pancras International through a subway under Pancras Road, with its entrance/exit within the central concourse.

The anticipated growth in passengers driven by the new Channel Tunnel Rail Link international and domestic train services, together with the generalised growth in the use of public transport in London, required an increase in passenger facilities at King's Cross St Pancras, primarily to provide new and additional capacity to the deep Tube line platforms and relieve pressure on the Tube ticket hall.

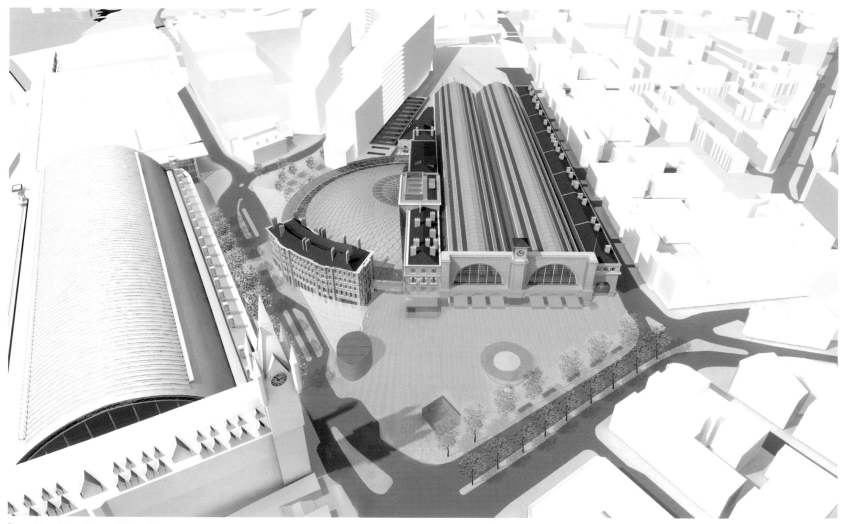

Planned London Underground/Network
Rail northern ticket hall, centre, from
above the Euston road looking north.

The new northern ticket hall will be a two-level structure, with a new King's Cross main line concourse sitting above it. It will be one storey below ground level with associated plant rooms underneath. New tunnelled passageways will connect to the existing platforms with escalators and lifts to all levels. The works to construct this new ticket hall will be completed in 2010, and are an essential component of London's public transport plan for the 2012 Olympic Games. A primary route for spectators to the Olympic Park at Stratford will be from St Pancras International on the Javelin service with a journey time of less than 10 minutes on the high-speed line.

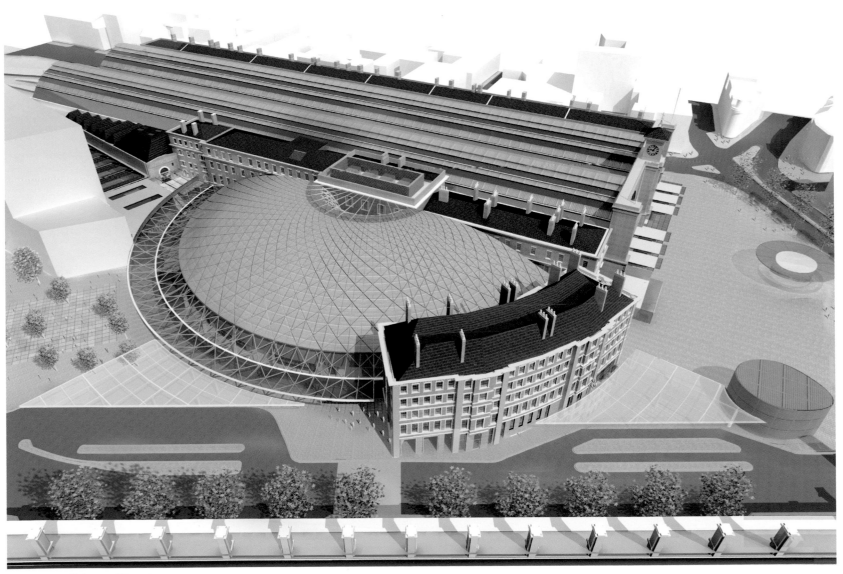

Planned London Underground/Network Rail northern ticket hall from above the St Pancras train shed looking east.

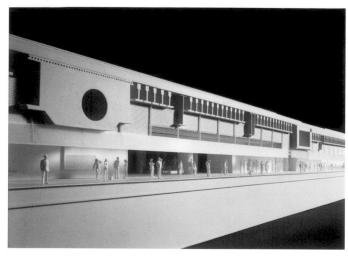

Longitudinal section through the First
Capital Connect station exposing
different thicknesses in the roof and
the position of the Fleet sewer.

A New First Capital Connect Station

A new station for 12-carriage First Capital Connect line trains, a service now operated by First Capital Connect, has been built beneath the western side of St Pancras. This new station is an essential element in the attraction and dispersal of passengers for the new St Pancras International station. The original King's Cross Thameslink station, situated on Pentonville Road, had become increasingly inadequate for the numbers of passengers passing through it. The new station has been constructed beneath Midland Road, on the western flank of St Pancras and on the existing alignment of the Midland City branch tunnel. It is integral with the foundation of the extended St Pancras International, with its entrance directly from the western end of the domestic concourse. Here lifts, stairs and escalators connect with the First Capital Connect platforms.

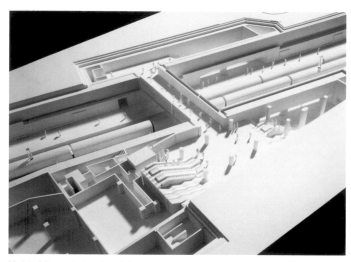

Model of the central portion of the
platforms and the footbridge of
the First Capital Connect station.

Escalator and staircase to the
First Capital Connect platforms.

Central concourse of the First Capital
Connect entrance looking north.

First Capital Connect intermediate
landing leading to the escalators.

First Capital Connect platform.

The design brief from London & Continental Railways was that every train-operating company using the new facilities should experience the same high quality of detailing and building finishes. The overall scale of the First Capital Connect subsurface station box is generous, and so the elements of the design respect the scale and magnitude of the structure. The walls comprise monumental precast concrete panels and are detailed to give the appearance of an engineered structural wall. A monolithic, plastered ceiling is suspended above the platform and occasionally acknowledges the grid of the station. Lighting, cameras and public announcement speakers are generally concealed behind two stainless-steel margins at the back of the platform located at ceiling level and at platform edge. Acoustically absorbent materials are housed vertically above this detail. Floor finishes at platform level are of terrazzo paving laid to reflect the station grid. The glazed wall and floor finishes, together with the colours used, unite these platforms with the rest of the main station above.

First Capital Connect connecting footbridge.

Main escalator group and lift from
intermediate landing to concourse.

The First Capital Connect line currently connects stations between Bedford and Brighton using a cross-London route that passes over the Thames at Blackfriars. London Gatwick Airport is less than an hour away to the south with Luton Airport just over half an hour to the north. Some 48 main line railway stations are directly served, including routes through Wimbledon and Sutton. A major upgrade and extension of the service, intended to more than double its present capacity, is under way. A junction built as part of the project at the north end of the station will enable additional services to operate over the Great Northern suburban lines to Cambridge and King's Lynn. St Pancras International will be at the very centre of this expanded network.

Platform escalators, stairs and lift to intermediate landing.

Midland Grand Hotel façade, Euston Road, with
departures gateway and clock tower, 2001.

Chapter 9
Renaissance of a Grand Hotel

Chapter 9
Renaissance of a Grand Hotel

The Midland Grand Hotel became St Pancras Chambers when the hotel closed in the 1930s, and was given over to utilitarian offices for the railway company which, in turn, abandoned the building in 1983 as being uneconomical to maintain. Although it was saved from demolition in 1967 by the 'Save St Pancras' campaign and listed as Grade I, it remained empty and deteriorating until 1993, when a major external renovation was undertaken by the British Rail Board to preserve and secure it, in the hope that at sometime a new use could be found for it. The exterior may have looked fine, but the interior was near derelict and had been crudely partitioned into office accommodation or

The Midland Grand Hotel, left foreground, from the corner of Judd Street and Euston Road looking north-east, before restoration.

George Gilbert Scott's drawing for the Euston Road façade: central oriel and dormer windows with crow step gable.

Midland Grand Hotel
double staircase.

left abandoned to the pigeons. The building, however, never failed to impress with its grand spaces and Gothic detailing.

In 1865 eleven architects were invited by the Midland Railway board to compete for the design of a large new hotel. This was to be the public face of St Pancras, London's most prestigious station. Among those competing, the following five were prominent architects: Edward Middleton Barry, George Somers Clarke, Owen Jones, George Gilbert Scott and Thomas Charles Sorby. Scott had been pressed to submit designs by a friend, Joseph Lewis, a Midland Railway director.

Midland Grand Hotel: main staircase
from an intermediate geometrical flight.

It is not difficult to see why Scott was chosen to design the Midland Grand Hotel. He was the best known of the competitors and had survived the extraordinary commotion surrounding his design for government offices in Whitehall. It is fair to say that he had not exactly triumphed — his design was rejected because of the anti-Gothic prejudice of Lord Palmerston. But he produced the final design for the Foreign Office — in a Renaissance style — and it was actually built. The whole episode was a baptism of fire for Scott, one from which few architects would have emerged unscathed. Scott, then, was tough, resilient and able to steer a difficult project through to ultimate success. He had probity, intellectual credibility and audacity. Like Allport, the managing director of the Midland Railway, Scott had published and lectured at the Royal Academy.

He tells us surprisingly little about the hotel in his *Recollections*, published in 1879 within months of his death on 27 March 1878. It would be a calumny, of course, to say that he merely recycled his rejected government offices design for the hotel. Here follow Scott's own words:

> July 11th, 1872
> I was persuaded . . . to enter into a limited competition for [the Midland Railway's] new terminus. I made my design while detained for several weeks with Mrs Scott by the severe illness of our son Alwynne, at a small seaside hotel in September and October 1865. I completely worked out the whole design then and made elevations to a large scale . . . The great shed-like roof had been already designed . . . as if by anticipation its section was a pointed arch . . . It is often spoken of to me as the finest building in London; my own belief is that it is possibly too good for its purpose, but having been disappointed . . . of my

Scott's drawing of the departures gateway and the tower. Unlike most Victorian architects, Scott executed very large drawings.

Building the Midland Grand Hotel, 1871, drawn by C. J. Richardson (1806–71). Richardson had been a pupil of Sir John Soane. This view from King's Cross looks across the soon-to-be-demolished Weston Place.

ardent hope of carrying out my style in the Government offices . . .
I was glad to be able to erect one building in that style in London . . .
(*Recollections*, 1879)

It is worth attempting to decode 'that style', as Scott put it. Clues are to be found in his *Remarks on Secular & Domestic Architecture Present and Future* (1857), a well-argued plea for the adoption of Gothic for the industrial age. There is only one illustration in the whole work: an engraved vignette on the title page. It is revealing. It shows four secular buildings: two representing the Gothic of the north and two the Gothic of the south. The gigantic cloth hall at Ypres, built between 1200 and 1304, and the medieval Palais de Justice in Liège are the northern representatives. The Gothic of the south is represented by the Palazzo Pubblico, Siena, built between 1297 and 1326, and the Doge's Palace, Venice, built between 1309 and 1424. The Venetian Palazzo Ducale was admired by authorities as diverse as Ruskin in his *Stones of Venice* (1851–53) and William Burges, the most sensual and mysterious of all the Gothic revivalists. Scott's Gothic was eclectic – a delectable, idiosyncratic, mingling of the north and south.

The 'large-scale elevations' that Scott executed in the hotel suite on Hayling Island have survived. They are in the Drawings Collection of the Royal Institute of British Architects. They were drawn when Scott would have been preoccupied by the rituals of Victorian illness – the daily visits of a doctor, a relay of nurses and the concerned attentions of Caroline, his wife. Alwynne, the sick son, was never strong and died at the age of twenty-nine. The four drawings of the façade of the Midland Grand Hotel are revealing. Scott – who had no difficulty with the mechanical, practical part of design – concentrated on the expressive elements of the building: entrances, gables and towers.

Scott's drawing of the proposed clock tower and spire, a remarkable competitor for Barry's Houses of Parliament clock tower in Westminster.

Contemporary perspective of the Midland Grand Hotel entrance, the departures gateway and the tower. Scott's secular Gothic is seen in its final form.

Drawing of the proposed ground-floor coffee lounge, dating from 1865. Like many such drawings, the grandeur of the room is exaggerated by making the people rather smaller.

Coffee saloon, as opened in 1873.

Sitting room with Gillo furniture, 1876.

Scott was indebted to Pugin, his exact contemporary, throughout his working life. He wrote in his *Recollections*: 'I did not know Pugin, but his image in my imagination was like my guardian angel, and I often dreamed that I knew him . . . had he done nothing else, he would have established his name for all future ages as the great reformer of architecture. His noble protest has been followed by others, and it is a proud thing to think of, that among those who follow out the gothic revival, the principle of truthfulness is universally acknowledged as their guiding star.' Truthfulness was a leitmotif in nineteenth-century architectural discourse.

For John Ruskin the implications of architecture for society were paramount. For him, the minds of the builders mattered more than the building. He believed his age was transforming workers into machines. Scott was essentially a pragmatist. He had no grand social agenda. He did not challenge the nature of his times. Scott was essentially a moderniser. Do not be confused by the Gothic clothing of his work.

Europe's Most Modern Hotel

The Midland Grand Hotel, completed in 1873, was the most modern hotel in Europe when it opened. A contemporary guidebook said, 'it stands without a rival . . . for palatial beauty, comfort, and convenience.' The building had cost £304,335, the decoration and fittings £49,000 and the furnishings £84,000. In total, this amounted to £437,335. What would be the equivalent amount today? This is difficult to answer given the variables involved in a calculation:

Top of Midland Grand Hotel double staircase with wall stencilling that replaced the original scheme in 1901.

Hotel entrance hall positioned
behind the Porte Cochère, 1876.

Porter using an electric trolley hauls supplies in front of
the north elevation and forecourt entrance of the hotel
which leads to a secondary staircase and the platforms.

The Midland Grand survived as a hotel until 1935,
with a café on the forecoourt facing the Euston Road.

price indexes, gross domestic product, weekly wages, relative costs of
materials, costs of professional services . . . It is still worth hazarding that
something between half a billion and a billion pounds was spent on the hotel.
A contemporary writer declared:

> The designs of the interior, as well as the apartments – some of which
> are embellished with almost regal splendour – were the production of
> Sir Gilbert Scott, afterwards assisted by Mr. Sang. [Friedrich Sang, a
> German decorative artist.] The colouring is rich and almost faultlessly
> pleasing and harmonious, producing a marked medieval character. The
> ceiling of the reading-room glows in an atmosphere of gold and colour,
> yet free and graceful in its figures and ornaments, designed by Mr.
> Sang. The large and magnificent coffee-room, the 'grand saloon',
> together with the adjoining 'state' and reception rooms, probably have
> no equal in point of design or finish in any building of the kind; while
> the corridors and staircases throughout are all decorated in a rich
> style, at once tasteful and beautiful.

The eastern wing of the Midland Grand Hotel was opened on 5 May 1873 and
the hotel was completed in the spring of 1876. For a decade, perhaps more,
the Midland Grand was the most modern hotel in London. It had hydraulic
passenger lifts – 'ascending chambers' – dust chutes on every floor, speaking
tubes, electric bells, suites of rooms, single rooms (cost close to an average
worker's weekly wage for a night's accommodation), a steam laundry,
previously undreamed-of fire precautions, geometrically patterned Minton
encaustic tiled floors of hallucinating complexity . . . The hotel prospered.

But the First World War damaged the hotel trade. By the 1920s the Midland
Grand was in the doldrums, seemingly fusty and old-fashioned. Several well-
known London hotels closed down. Refurbishing the Midland was unthinkable.
Victorian taste had no defenders. Le Corbusier's brilliantly polemical *Vers une
Architecture* (1923), translated as *Towards a New Architecture* in 1927, made
people feel there was something morally suspect about decorated, historicist
buildings. The Midland Grand survived as a hotel – extraordinarily – until
1935, for 62 years. Then it was transformed into the London, Midland &
Scottish Railway offices. But, after all, hotels are rather like ocean liners –
their lifespans are usually no more than two, or at the most three, decades.
Posterity will thank us for giving new life to Scott's extraordinary masterpiece.

Basement: below stairs in the Midland Grand Hotel. Pipes, wires
and services and a fire hose cabinet with linen fold panelling.

Entrance hall: tiled flooring with the concierge's office and
passageways to the dining room and main staircase.

First floor: T. Wallis Hay's mural *The Garden of Deduit*
in the niche and the first-floor landing to the right.

Second floor: light-well bringing natural illumination through the
centre of the building from the fifth down to the first floor.

New Life for a Grand Hotel

The former Midland Grand Hotel (St Pancras Chambers since 1935) is being reborn as part of the renaissance of St Pancras.

London & Continental Railways (LCR) was keen to ensure that the hotel building should once again have a viable and sustainable use, one that could justify and afford the necessary and extensive refurbishment. The building's Euston Road elevation is, after all, the public face of the international station. By marketing the opportunity and running a developer competition LCR was able to secure the interest of Manhattan Loft Corporation (MLC) and Marriott Hotels to redevelop Scott's magnificent Midland Grand Hotel.

Above: Former coffee lounge as taken over by London & Continental Railways. The ragged-edged change of colour of the walls indicates the level of a false ceiling installed to save fuel costs.

Right: The Midland Grand Hotel reflected in the windows of the British Library on the other side of Midland Road.

Proposed ground-floor restaurant.

Proposed loft apartment.

MLC was successful where others had failed by combining the hotel with apartments. The hotel will have 244 bedrooms, restaurants, two bars, a health and leisure centre, a ballroom, meeting rooms and business centres, as well as 67 new apartments in the upper levels. The building is to be renamed the St Pancras Renaissance Hotel and will be a five-star flagship of the Marriott Renaissance hotel brand.

MLC's early deliberations concluded with the need to build a new wing adjacent to the hotel and on top of the newly constructed west side buildings on Midland Road. The main reason for the new addition was to make the development economically viable – the extra wing extended the hotel providing the critical mass of hotel bedrooms, and allowed residential apartments to be developed within the loft area that had been the servants' quarters as well as on the upper floors of the original hotel. All the internal rooms of historic significance will be restored to their former glory with appropriate public access.

The first response of RHWL Architects, who were commissioned by MLC, was to distinguish the new building from the design of the newly constructed podium. They suggested putting two stacks of rooms, slightly staggered, like passing trains, in a glass box. Their design was a brave effort but English Heritage ruled it out and insisted that the hotel wing be in the 'Scott manner'. Richard Griffiths, who was already working with MLC and RHWL as their conservation adviser on aspects of the Midland Grand Hotel scheme, was asked to design the façade of the building.

After several schemes that involved working around the complicated structural constraints of the site, a consensus was achieved, determined by English Heritage's desire to build in the Scott manner. The new design certainly borrows from Scott's composition of the front of St Pancras, which has two layers of pointed windows and a zone of triple-arched windows terminating in attic rooms placed within a steep roof.

George Gilbert Scott, 1860s.

Sir George Gilbert Scott (1811–78)

George Gilbert Scott was the fourth child of Thomas Scott (1780–1834), the impecunious Perpetual Curate of Gawcott, a village a mile south-west of the small market town of Buckingham, and his wife Euphemia, *née* Lynch (1786–1854). In order to supplement his modest stipend, Thomas Scott ran an academy from his vicarage. It was, in actuality, a school that adults who 'wished to read for the church' also attended. Scott claimed that he learnt little at his father's academy, and wrote in his autobiography, *Personal and Professional Recollections*: 'The defects of my education have been like a millstone about my neck and have made me almost dread superior society.' As an adolescent, Scott wandered about the countryside making sketches of medieval buildings. Recognising his talent for architecture, the Rev. Scott arranged for lessons in drawing – from an artist who had attracted the attention of Joshua Reynolds. Scott's uncle later taught him mathematics and the rudiments of classical architecture.

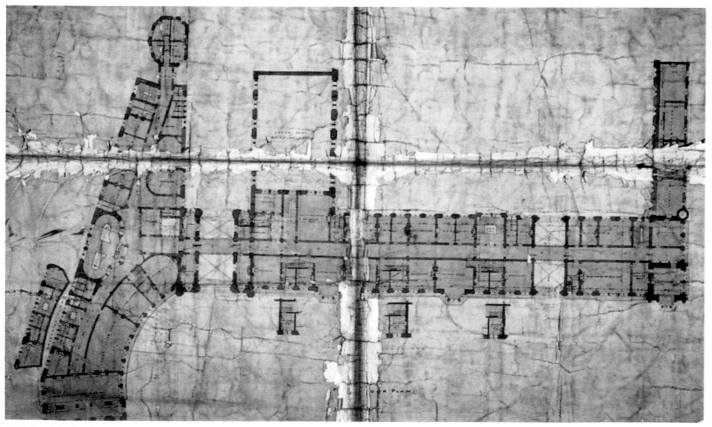

1866 plan of the first floor of the Midland Grand Hotel showing the bridges across the departures gateway, left, and the arrivals gateway, right.

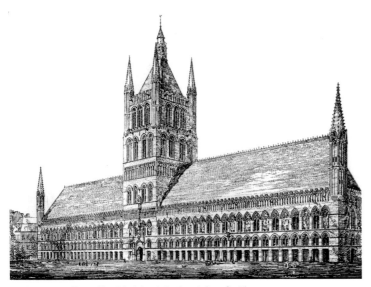

The Cloth Hall at Ypres (Flemish, Lakenhalle, Ieper), from Scott's, *Lectures on the rise and development of mediaeval architecture*, 1879. Scott visited Flanders in 1847 to study Flemish Gothic en route for Germany where he was working on his Nikolaikirche, Hamburg (1844–60). The influence of the greatest surviving medieval secular building is apparent in the Midland Grand Hotel.

At sixteen, Scott was articled to an architect, James Edmeston, a 'kindly' man – who disliked Gothic. He designed in what Scott called the 'debased style of 1827. . . a mere blank-sheet as to matters of taste . . .' On completing his articles, Scott worked for a leading building contractor. He was briefly to share an office with Sampson Kempthorne (1809–73) who had designed a cheap standardised, workhouse for the Poor Law Commissioners. At the age of twenty-three Scott set up his own practice. He later formed a partnership with William Bonython Moffatt (1812–87), a fellow pupil of Edmeston. The partnership was to last for 11 years. With Moffatt, he designed some 50 workhouses, several lunatic asylums and a prison – 'dirty, disagreeable work,' he said. Scott, however, became impressed with the ideas of Pugin who presented the case for Gothic in a witty and easily assimilated form – notably in his *Contrasts* of 1836. Scott was to reiterate Pugin's arguments in his *Remarks on Secular & Domestic Architecture Present and Future* (1857).

Despite the uninspiring nature of the work in the Scott Moffatt office, Scott taught himself how to design in the Gothic manner. He became a subscriber to the *Ecclesiologist* (1841–69), an influential journal published by the Cambridge Camden Society. The society was concerned with revitalising the

1866 elevation of the Midland Grand Hotel.

The Albert Memorial, London, by George Gilbert Scott, 1863–72,
with the statue of Albert seated in 1875 and unveiled in 1876.
With more than 175 statues of writers, musicians and architects,
together with groups representing the four continents, the memorial
reveals the Victorian psyche at its most confident. The seated figure
of Prince Albert is by Joseph Durham, 1814–77. Scott's design
was inspired by the medieval aedicule – a miniature building
designed to house a vessel containing the consecrated host.

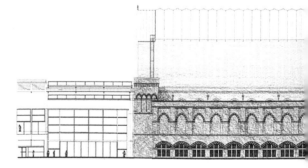

Anglican Church and was inclined to conflate architecture with religion. Catholic ethics had provided the inspiration for the wonderful architecture of the Middle Ages – it was hoped that, by a process of reverse osmosis, 'Catholick architecture will give rise to Catholick ethics'. Scott was to remain committed to the Gothic cause for the remainder of his life long after the tide had turned against it.

Scott's first great architectural success, while he was still in partnership with Moffatt, came with the acceptance of his design for the Nikolaikirche, Hamburg (1844–60). It was the tallest building in the world for some time. The nave was destroyed by Allied bombs on 28 July 1943 but Scott's tower survives – a reminder of the indiscriminate barbarity of war. Among Scott's other important buildings were the Italianate Foreign and India Offices in Whitehall (1860 onwards), in association with Matthew Digby Wyatt (1820–77) – Scott had been obliged to jettison his original Gothic design upon the insistence of Lord Palmerston – and the Albert Memorial, which was completed in 1875. Scott had a high reputation during his lifetime for his work as a restorer of cathedrals and abbeys: Ely (1848–70), Westminster Abbey

(1849–78), St David's (1862–78), etc. His approach to restoration has been criticised by later generations, but it must be remembered that he was a pioneer in the art of restoration. Appreciation is more appropriate than condemnation.

Scott's eldest son, George Gilbert Scott, junior (1839–97), a gifted architect, became a Roman Catholic and designed what is now the Catholic Cathedral of Norwich. He was an alcoholic and died in his father's Midland Grand Hotel. Scott's best-known pupil was George Edmund Street (1824–81), the designer of the Royal Courts of Justice in The Strand, opened in 1882.

After Scott's death, his firm passed to his second son John Oldrid Scott (1841–1915) and later to his grandson, Sir Giles Gilbert Scott (1880–1960), the architect of Liverpool's Anglican Cathedral, Battersea Power Station, Bankside Power Station – now Tate Modern – and the red cast-iron telephone box.

Scott was knighted in 1872 and served as president of the Royal Institute of British Architects from 1873 to 1875. He was buried in Westminster Abbey and his memorial plaque was designed by his pupil George Edmund Street.

A drawing by Richard Griffiths Architects showing the newly constructed lower podium and upper-level blind brick arches to the north. Designed in close conjunction with English Heritage and the London Borough of Camden by the Rail Link Engineering architectural team, it pays homage to George Gilbert Scott's original design. The new wing for the extended St Pancras Chambers echoes the same architectural logic, providing two floors of bedrooms into a single storey order. The remaining bulk of the hotel, however, borrows from Scott's composition from the south elevation of the Chambers.

Two new bridges crossing the Regent's Canal give access to public space between a restored heritage railway and canal building converted for new commercial and residential uses.

Chapter 10
A New Heart for London

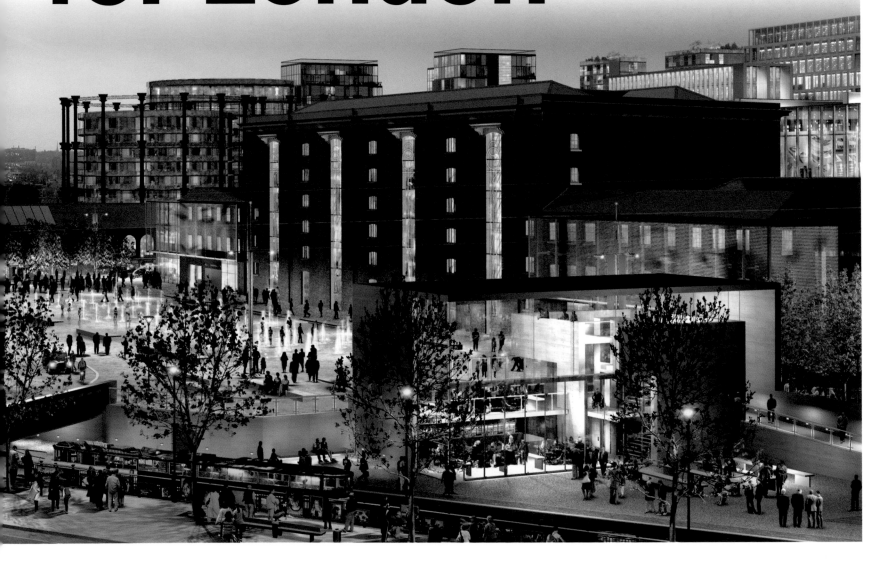

A New Heart for London

The arrival of the Midland Railway and St Pancras station to sit alongside King's Cross in 1868 caused social upheaval on a scale unseen in London. The suburban expansion of north London in the area had taken place in the 1820s and 1830s. Wherever a new city terminus was to be built it invariably required the demolition of existing property. St Pancras was prevented from getting any closer to the centre of London by the decision of the Metropolitan Railway Termini Commissioners in 1846, who decided against any further surface railways from north of London having termini south of the Euston Road. St Pancras, therefore, was sited against the northern side of the Euston Road. This required the houses, shacks and hovels of Agar Town to be demolished together with businesses and shops that lined the network of streets, alleys and back passages between Old Pancras Road (now Pancras Road) and Skinners and Brewers Streets (now Midland Road, out of deference to the Midland Railway).

Research has shown that the decrepitude of Agar Town, required by the Midland Railway in order to secure parliamentary approval and public acceptance of the building of their London terminal terminal at St Pancras, was exaggerated. The area was undoubtedly poor but was comparable to Somers Town on the Euston Road. The dispersal of the inhabitants from land required for St Pancras station led to the subsequent requirement that the Midland Railway rehouse those who were displaced from Somers Town by the building of the adjacent goods depot. Some of the new multistorey blocks had Midland Railway attendants.

Frederick Williams in *The Midland Railway: Its Rise and Progress* provides us with a selective and overly colourful account of the coming off the Midland Railway to Agar Town:

> For its passenger station alone it swept away a church and seven streets of three thousand houses. Old St Pancras churchyard was invaded, and Agar Town almost demolished . . . the place a very 'abomination of desolation' . . . occupied by knackers' yards . . . At the broken doors of mutilated houses canaries still sang, and dogs lay basking in the sun, as if to remind one of the vast colonies of bird-fanciers and dog-fanciers who formerly made Agar Town their abode; and from these dwellings came out wretched creatures in rags and dirt . . . while over the whole neighbourhood the gas-works poured forth their mephitic vapours, and the canal gave forth its rheumatic dampness . . . Such was Agar Town before the Midland Railway came into the midst of it.

The much altered and renovated church beside the station. St Pancras was made prebendal manor by King Ethelbert and part of lands given to St Paul's Cathedral around the year 603 and a parish before the Norman Conquest in 1066. The place was called 'Pancras' in the Domesday Book in 1086.

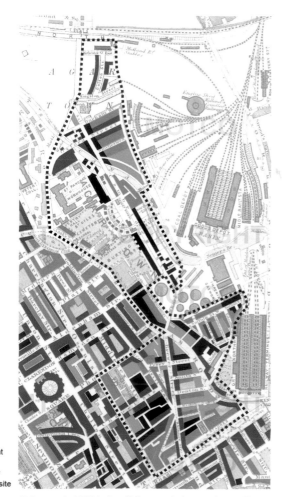

Key to map:

■ poorest

■
■
■
■
■
■

■ most affluent

•••• boundary of St Pancras site

St Pancras in 1866, before St Pancras station and Somers Town were built by the Midland Railway, showing the relative poverty and affluence in the area, back-projected using the mapping techniques of Charles Booth in his survey of London, 1886–1903.

Temporary bridge to the north of the station with an embankment constructed over the graveyard of St Pancras Old Church, *Illustrated London News*, 16 March 1867. This was the first of many incursions into the burial grounds of St Pancras church, St George's Bloomsbury and St Giles churches.

Hardy's Tree in Old St Pancras churchyard.

To build St Pancras station, 'Old St Pancras churchyard was invaded' Williams blithely tells us. Thomas Hardy, while a pupil architect in his mid-twenties, was delegated to see that the exhumation of mouldering corpses from the churchyard was carried out with respect for the dead before their bones were reburied.

Seventeen years after the grisly destruction of Old St Pancras churchyard Hardy, now settled in Wimborne, Dorset, and having abandoned architecture, wrote:

O Passenger, pray list and catch
Our sighs and piteous groans,
Half stifled in this jumbled patch
Of wrenched memorial stones!

We late-lamented, resting here,
Are mixed to human jam,
And each to each exclaims in fear,
'I know not which I am!'

The wicked people have annexed
The verses on the good;
A roaring drunkard sports the text
Teetotal Tommy should!

Where we are huddled none can trace,
And if our names remain,
They pave some path or porch or place
Where we have never lain!

Here's not a modest maiden elf
But dreads the final Trumpet,
Lest half of her should rise herself,
And half some sturdy strumpet!

From restorations of Thy fane,
From smoothings of Thy sward,
From zealous Churchmen's pick and plane
Deliver us O Lord! Amen!

The Levelled Churchyard, 1881.

London going out of Town, the March of Bricks and Mortar, satire by George Cruikshank,1829.

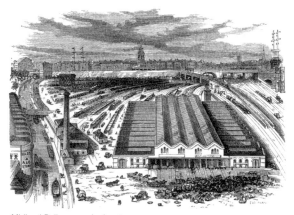

Midland Railway goods depot built on Agar Town and beside the Regent's Canal, 1877.

St Pancras and King's Cross, June 1957. There are extensive railway lands to the north and Somers Town goods depot to the west.

Dispossessed Church

Providing sufficient church places for the 'huddled masses' living on the site was a constant worry for the Church of England. A newspaper notice appealing for funds for St Luke's Church, Euston Road, pointed out: 'This district contains a population of nearly 10,000 souls, and is scarcely to be paralleled in the metropolis for abject poverty, gross ignorance and utter spiritual destitution. The number of shops opened every Lord's-day for purposes of traffic far exceeds the number of those, which are closed'. The irony of the situation for the Church was compounded by the fact that the freeholders of the land upon which this dereliction stood were the Ecclesiastical Commissioners.

By 1861, the housing facing on to the Euston Road had itself been rebuilt to a better standard and included the relocated and permanent St Luke's Church built between the rows of houses. It had been an 'iron' church made of a demountable frame covered with corrugated sheeting and had started life as St Paul's, Camden Square. As that area acquired a more permanent edifice so the building moved first to the grounds of the smallpox hospital, with permission of the directors of the Great Northern Railway, as St Luke's, King's Cross, and then became the forerunner of a permanent stone church, St Luke's in Euston Road. After years of inactivity due to lack of funds the stone church had been finished in May 1861. It was on the site for just 15 months before the Midland Railway received powers to acquire it along with the housing described above. In compensation, the railway had to pay for the building of St Luke's Church, Oseney Crescent, Kentish Town.

The materials of St Luke's Church, Euston Road, were sold (except for the brickwork which was required for the new buildings) as the church was no longer needed, the parish having disappeared. Its stone and timber fittings were carted 14.5 kilometres (9 miles) to Wanstead, where, over 130 years later, a slightly smaller church still serves United Reformed Church members in Nightingale Lane.

The St Pancras area remained poor after the building of the station. Blocks of tenement flats were built by the Improved Industrial Dwellings Company in the 1860s – Pevsner described them as 'horrible'. For all their meagre comforts, they must actually have been preferable to the 'mutilated' houses of which Williams spoke. One of these tenement blocks – one of the Stanley Buildings – is to be preserved. Alexander Mackendrick's *The Ladykillers* (1955), a hilarious but sinister film of bungled crime, captures the earlier atmosphere of the St Pancras area. In very recent memory, King's Cross St Pancras had elements that were associated with all that is unsavoury in life. St Pancras International is the catalyst that will transform it.

The King's Cross, 1836 by G. S. Shepherd. The monument, which gave the district its name, celebrated the reign of George IV, the former Prince Regent.

Demolition of King's Cross,1845, looking east towards Pentonville Road, left, and Gray's Inn Road, right.

Rebirth of an Area

The building of the two adjacent stations is only part of the story as termini invariably required large areas for rolling-stock stabling and cleaning, as well as sidings, turntables and engine sheds for the maintenance of the locomotives. Additionally, merchandise was also carried as close to the terminus as possible, or at least as far as a suitable transhipment point. In the case of both King's Cross and St Pancras, these ancillary facilities were located to the north of the Regent's Canal. The area came to be known as the railway lands and occupied over 27 hectares (67 acres). Few rights of way across the sites were present when the railways came and therefore few bridges were erected to perpetuate these rights.

Why King's Cross?

Even today, property developers think deeply about the name to be given to their latest enterprise. 'King's Cross' is the result of serendipity. The original name given to the area was Battle Bridge, as it was the supposed site of a battle in AD 61 between Boudicca, the ruler of the Iceni Brythonic Celtic tribe in East Anglia and the Roman Seutonius Paulinus.

According to Gavin Stamp in *From Battle Bridge to King's Cross*, 'W. Forrester Bray, builder of the first houses on the Battle Bridge estate, toyed with calling the area "Boudicca's Cross" or "St. George's Cross" until the advent of the free-standing structure at the road junction bearing the statue of George IV provided a name with Royal cachet'. The statue of the king was erected in 1836 (the king had died in 1830) and it and the plinth on which it stood were disliked for a number of reasons. George IV was the subject of much gossip and political satire due to his matrimonial arrangements and his gluttony. Monuments to George IV were rare and became rarer still after the St Pancras Vestry (the local authority until 1900) removed the obelisk at King's Cross in 1845 because it was a 'public nuisance'. It had lasted less than ten years. The structure was not unpleasant in itself, but probably obstructed the increasing traffic as well as commemorating an unpopular monarch.

The name King's Cross has been adopted by this part of London for good or ill, and the area is now being given a renewed cachet through the redevelopment of the former railway lands to the north of St Pancras and King's Cross stations. No call for the replication of the actual Cross though, yet.

Granary Square, Kings Cross Central. Looking north across the canal towards the Granary.

Pancras Square, King's Cross Central.

Eurostar services started operating out of St Pancras International on 14 November 2007, and we can now look forward to the long awaited £2bn-plus regeneration of the area behind the stations, a development known as King's Cross Central. This swathe of land, which has lain blighted for many years, provides a unique opportunity to develop what is the largest, and most accessible, plot of derelict and underused land in central London. The development will therefore fundamentally change the social and economic character of the King's Cross area.

The site is owned and controlled jointly by London & Continental Railways (LCR), the promoter of the Channel Tunnel Rail Link project, and DHL-Exel Supply Chain (DHL-Exel), an international logistics company.

LCR has been working with DHL-Exel for a number of years and both companies were former board members of the King's Cross Partnership, which operated from 1996 until 2003 with the aim of transforming the King's Cross area into a vibrant and successful part of London.

In 2001, the landowners entered into a joint venture agreement with Argent Group plc (Argent), one of the United Kingdom's most respected property development companies. Argent has built a reputation on successful city-centre regeneration schemes, notably Brindleyplace in Birmingham and the ongoing rejuvenation of Piccadilly in central Manchester.

King's Cross Central

The vision is now in place and has been spectacularly modelled, showing how 27 hectares (67 acres) of underused land with a rich and historic legacy, and the best public transport access in London will be transformed into a dense and distinctive urban quarter, integrated with one of the busiest transport interchanges in the western hemisphere: King's Cross Central.

The scale of development, the mix of land uses, its central London location and transport links mean that King's Cross Central is one of the most important development and regeneration projects in London. It will deliver a fundamental change to the economy and environment of this key part of central London, redefining current images of King's Cross and producing substantial benefits for the community, locally and across London.

Planning permission was granted in December 2006 for the main site – some 715,350 square metres (7.7 million square feet) of mixed-use space. The plans include up to 455,220 square metres (4.9 million square feet) of office/workspace, 1,900 new homes and up to 45,985 square metres (495,000 square feet) of shopping, food and drink, plus a hotel, serviced apartments and student accommodation; augmented by leisure, health, cultural, community and educational uses. The 50 new buildings that will complement 20 refurbished historic buildings and structures will be set

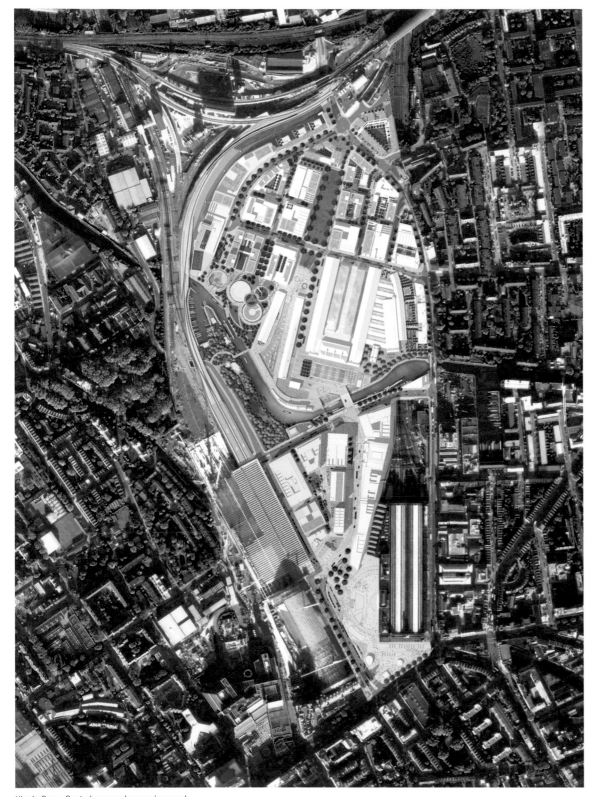

King's Cross Central proposals superimposed
on a satellite image of the railway lands north
of St Pancras and King's Cross stations.

Simulation of Cubitt Park,
King's Cross Central.

around high-quality and genuinely public new streets and squares. Over 40 per cent of the development will be for the public realm, including ten new public spaces, 20 new streets and three new bridges over the Regent's Canal. All in all, there will be some 11 hectares (27 acres) of public realm, to be managed to world-class standards.

The surrounding neighbourhoods of Somers Town, Cooper's Lane and Ampthill Square to the west, Agar Grove and Maiden Lane to the north, and Market Road, the Bemerton Estates and Naish Court to the east include areas of long-standing social deprivation, not aided by the historic severance of communities generated by the original development of the stations and goods depots. Physical, social and economic integration between the new development and its surrounding communities has been a key objective, and therefore one that has conditioned the project from the very beginning. This physical integration includes a new hierarchy of streets and footpaths permeating through the site and linking it to the east and west. Links to the local Underground and train stations, enhancements to the Regent's Canal and funding for improvements to local bus routes will also be provided and opportunities for the Cross River Tram will be anticipated.

Triplet gas holder guide frames
re-erected with residential units.

Goods Street, King's Cross Central.

The development is at the forefront of efforts to address climate change. It is high density and mixed use, with low parking levels, urban 'home zones' and a range of commitments to extending walking, cycling and public transport. There is a commitment to reducing carbon emissions by at least 39 per cent, compared with the 'business as usual' benchmark, through reducing energy demand, supplying energy efficiently and incorporating the use of renewable energy sources. In addition, there will be a Carbon Fund to support the application of new technologies.

The result will be not just stylish new offices and homes, and the familiar high street brands, but a serious commitment to place-making. King's Cross Central will retain some of its urban 'grittiness' but will also be clean, safe and provided with excellent facilities. The investment in the site is set to follow over the next 12 to 15 years, including a substantial first phase by 2010. New public ways through the proposed development will allow the newly created urban fabric to be woven into that to the east and west of the area.

St Pancras International and King's Cross Central are set to provide a vibrant new heart for London with twenty-first-century architecture and transport connections, while retaining the best of the area's historic past.

Great Northern Hotel, attached to King's Cross station, **out of picture right**, by the northern ticket hall's Arcade canopy.

Eastern extension entrance and transition roof, 2007.

Chapter 11
A Place to Meet

A Place to Meet

A hundred and forty years ago, St Pancras was the most modern station in the world. It is once more. The railway has come into its own again. St Pancras International links two masterpieces. Barlow and Ordish's magnificent train shed was the most advanced building of its age. It is joined to Sir George Gilbert Scott's hotel which, for all its medieval aspect, was the prototype of the modern luxury hotel. Now, little more than two hours' journey away by Eurostar, is another masterpiece: Jacques Ignace Hittorff's supremely elegant, Grecian Gare du Nord in Paris. This was once the height of nineteenth-century modernity – it, too, has been revivified. There can be no comparable architectural experience in travelling from one great capital to another. History and modernity are seamlessly joined. Railway termini are microcosms. They are, in many ways, the contemporary equivalent of the medieval cathedral. Our world is more complex than the medieval world – and it is never static. The great station must serve our needs. A modern station needs banks, bureaux de change, bars, restaurants. And it must have shops. St Pancras International now serves the needs of travellers in the way of the most sophisticated transport hubs.

St Pancras in use again, 14 November 2007.

Night in the train shed looking north.

Lighting at Night

With its newly glazed roof, St Pancras is filled with light during the day. Most railway stations are lit downwards. At night – with their intimidating, cavernous roof spaces – they are invariably dismal and alienating. However, St Pancras takes on a new life at night. As daylight fades, the new lighting system comes into play. This transition takes place gradually and imperceptibly. It is one of the most intriguing sights of contemporary London.

Barlow and Ordish's roof structure is among the most gracious ever constructed. Nothing of comparable age survives. The lighting scheme makes it possible to see its wrought-iron construction as it has never been seen before – once more in the tranquil blue colour scheme approved by Scott. Platforms are lit by a continuous lighting catenary that provides a pleasant level of lighting for departing and arriving passengers.

Catenary-lit platform looking north.

Arup designed the lighting catenary. The structures supporting it also incorporate passenger information displays, security cameras, fire alarm points and call points. The lighting units, which are up to 50 metres (164 feet) in length, also house speakers for passenger announcements; these are approximately 6 metres (19 feet 6 inches) apart. The disagreeable and often barely comprehensible announcements heard on the traditional station address systems are thus avoided. The west side of the train shed is treated as a concourse for passenger and public circulation. Here illumination is more intense.

Extension looking north at night.

Above and facing page: Day, twilight and night looking north from the first floor of the Midland Grand Hotel.

The principal brief to designers was to reveal the noble structure of the Barlow–Ordish train shed – and at the same time provide pleasing ambient lighting throughout the station. The aim was to avoid reflections or shadows at platform level. The models were I. M. Pei's Pyramid at the Musée du Louvre in Paris (1989), and Colin St John Wilson's British Library (1997), next door to St Pancras. Claude Engle III was responsible for the lighting of these two buildings. Based in Chevy Chase, Maryland, Engle is probably the world's best-known authority on lighting. He was responsible for the spectacular inverted cone of mirrors that vastly increased the level of natural lighting in Forster's Berlin Reichstag. Engle was consulted over the lighting of St Pancras. A unique solution was devised to create an even distribution of uplighting by lights situated on the upper side of the catenary units.

Top: twilight and **above:** night.

The quality of light on the western side at platform level.

Corber, the joint-venture contractor responsible for the lighting of St Pancras, has taken the lighting programme yet further. The company has developed a system in which there is interplay between the varieties of subsidiary lighting systems. To add to the problems of lighting a very large internal space, there are the secondary reflections generated by the terrazzo floors, glass walls and, not least, nineteenth-century brickwork – now, with almost a century and a half of grime removed, as bright as it was on the day the station first opened. Lit by one of the most advanced lighting systems in existence St Pancras is one of the most impressive of all enclosed spaces.

The lighting scheme is another major St Pancras achievement.

The quality of light on terrazzo flooring and glass walls.

Signage

Until the 1990s, all British railway stations had similar signage. Signs proclaimed 'Exit', 'Information' and so forth. Passenger information was displayed in a similar way. All conformed to British Rail's standards of corporate identity. BR's signage was efficient enough, but over the years it had come to seem dowdy. By the mid-1990s the design of stations, and passenger needs and aspirations had changed beyond measure.

St Pancras is a complex station. It is also very large. As it is one of the world's great international termini, clear signage is of paramount importance. From among the mass of visual data that assails the eye, signs must assert themselves. There must be a hierarchy of signs. First the general: 'Departure' and 'Arrival'. Then the particular: 'Bureau de Change', 'Information' and so forth. Signs must be instantly readable – and readable from a distance. Above all, signs need authority and the gravitas to convey crucial information.

The St Pancras International logotype announces the station to passengers arriving on the eastern side of the east–west concourse.

All St Pancras visual and textual information has been very carefully planned. Location of signage, typeface, pictographic signs – which transcend verbal language – colour and size of lettering must all be taken into account. For a station of the international importance of St Pancras, design consultants specialising in transport design were engaged to advise on signage. Although St Pancras is one of the great, perhaps the greatest, surviving examples of nineteenth-century modernity, a pastiche typographical style for such an advanced station was not appropriate. There were also the new Stratford and Ebbsfleet stations that had to be taken into consideration. Bruno Maag of Dalton Maag, the Swiss-trained but now London-based typographical designer, was commissioned to design a typeface specifically for St Pancras International. Maag's typeface is appropriately called 'Barlow'. The blue and yellow colouring of the signage – Eurostar's colours – is a constant and delightful reminder of Eurostar's association with the St Pancras project.

Barlow
abcdefghijklmnopqrstuvwxyz
ABCDEFGHIJKLMNOPQRSTUVWXYZ
0123456789

Barlow font designed for St Pancras and
the other High Speed 1 line stations.

Barlow font in Eurostar's blue and yellow.

Directional signage in the undercroft, where beer barrels were once stored, posed a challenge to designers. The undercroft – the busiest part of the station – has, by the standards of large public spaces, a comparatively low ceiling height. Then there is the multiplicity of columns. In other words, there is less than the usual space in which to display important and sometimes complex information. To fit between the columns the maximum sign panel length is 1,700 millimetres (67 inches) and all panels are positioned at 2,800 millimetres (110 inches) above floor level. These line up with the top of the cruciform brackets – or capitals – on the original Barlow cast-iron columns.

A crucial aspect of the signage, driven by the complex layout of St Pancras International, has been the inclusion of train operator branding. Each train

Signs line up with the brackets on William Henry Barlow's cast-iron columns.

East Midland signage in the
extension, looking north.

Passenger information point.

Signage in The Arcade.

operator has principal use of a group of platforms. This makes possible the indication of a virtual 'portal' indicating operators' areas of the station. Although it is desirable to use platform numbers to direct passengers to their correct trains, it was also clear that most passengers would be aware of the train operator running the service they wanted to use. The portals themselves are clearly identified using the operators' brand graphics, together with the names in the directional signage.

As a further aid to the traveller, train information displays are located around the station and inside the shops, cafés, bars and restaurants, so that travellers can feel comfortable that they have up-to-the-minute information about their train service.

Signage on the east–west concourse for the different train operators.

A Destination Station

Shops bring life and energy to airports and to stations. In the case of
St Pancras International, the public – not merely travellers – will shop in
the new undercroft. Fitting modern shops into an exceptional Grade I listed
building has had to be handled with considerable sensitivity. English Heritage
and the London Borough of Camden were, quite rightly, eager to review
designs specifically covering retail premises, signage and advertising. They
were concerned that the introduction of retail could undermine the historic
integrity of a great building.

The Arcade in the former undercroft and Rendezvous at platform level were
the first areas to be considered. At platform level, drawings showed 15 new
openings through the west side wall and the existing openings at platform
level. The setting called for traditional timber, part-glazed doors that matched
the original doors at this level.

The doors on the west of the station take their details from the existing
doors on the south end of the east side buildings. They are of varnished oak.
The hand-wrought brass escutcheons and hinges – said to look like 'a court
jester's hat' – replicate those on the former booking hall doors. George Gilbert
Scott's office specialised in metalwork; his screen for Hereford Cathedral,
made in 1862 by Skidmore of Coventry, is now one of the treasures of the V&A.
It is among the finest examples of Victorian metalwork. Scott's brasswork,
jewel-like and unfamiliar to our eyes, reminds us, at the microscale, of the
wonderful, complex age that first brought St Pancras into being.

Platform-level door furniture.

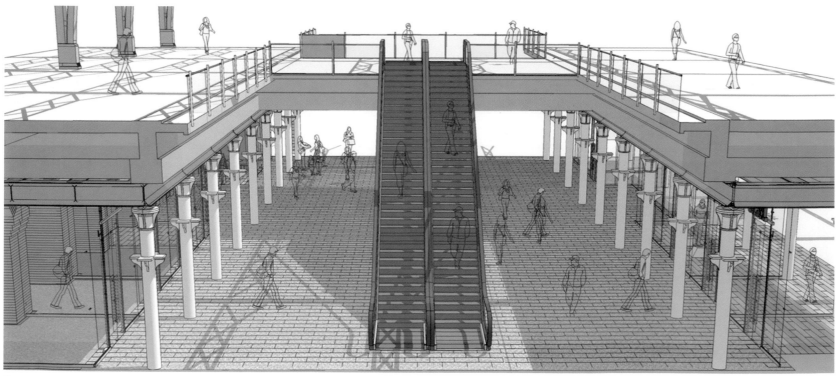

The Arcade looking north.

Customers enjoying the The Arcade.

The Arcade, at undercroft level, presented different challenges. Its west side consists of a series of blind brick arches. With the agreement of English Heritage and the London Borough of Camden, the brickwork has been removed and replaced with frameless glass shopfronts. Elsewhere the shopfronts project from this plane of brickwork and form uniform bays of frameless glazing. The model was Burlington Arcade with its identical shop fronts, irrespective of the nature of individual businesses. English Heritage and the London Borough of Camden favoured this approach as it created a disciplined uniformity for the retail units. The opposite side of The Arcade, although not arched, adopted the same language of large frameless glass shopfronts. These are set back from the existing columns and aligned with the beam soffit of Barlow's ironwork. The original cast-iron columns now form a colonnade in front of the shop units within The Arcade.

Platform-level champagne bar,
The Arcade below, looking north.

Concourse of Grand Central Station, New York, re-opened after restoration, 2003.

The Arcade, with the champagne bar above, looking towards the south gable of the train shed.

A team that included Brandstory – leading branding experts – as marketing consultants has developed London and Continental Stations and Property's vision for the shopping experience at St Pancras.

The Brandstory strategy was to exploit the fantastic architecture of the station. Moreover, at the same time, they were to set high standards for customer service. This would create an environment where commerce could flourish and travellers would feel at ease and able to enjoy shopping. St Pancras is intended to be a destination in its own right – a place attractive to travellers and non-travellers alike.

London and Continental Stations and Property (LCSP), responsible for the marketing of St Pancras, was determined to find out who its customers were and what services and quality standards they really wanted. Research was carried out among Eurostar and domestic customers – and Londoners – to determine what brands would draw them to the station.

Studies of successful shopping venues at airports and stations were undertaken. St Pancras, it was intended, would have shopping facilities to equal or surpass those at any airport. Amsterdam's Schiphol Airport, which handles nearly 50 million passengers a year, was an obvious exemplar to study. It is often described as 'the best airport in the world'. Its shopping piazza is much admired. Among stations studied were Rome's Stazione Termini and New York's Grand Central. The Stazione Termini, built in 1950, had iconic status among post-war architects. Its concrete expanse still impresses. Within a comparatively limited concourse area it manages to house excellent facilities. Grand Central, completed in 1913 by Warren and Wetmore, is among the best examples of the American École des Beaux Arts style. Like St Pancras, it was saved from destruction by a lively public campaign. It was restored in 1994 and is one of the most inspiring of urban renewal projects. This is probably the principal inspiration for the revitalised St Pancras. Grand Central is now a popular meeting place for New Yorkers: there are five restaurants and a notable cocktail lounge. The characteristics of popular shopping streets – like Marylebone High Street, with its delightfully eclectic mix of sophisticated shops – were also studied.

A strategy was established: the creation of spaces that would be attractive to commercial tenants as well as to a wide range of customers. Four distinct zones have been created:

The Circle: Meets the needs of regular commuters in a convenient way. Well-known high street brands are clustered together: Marks & Spencer – the first full Marks & Spencer at any station – and Boots, with a new concept store. There are also W. H. Smith, Prêt à Manger, Monsoon, Leon and Yo! Sushi – the authentic Japanese conveyor-belt restaurant chain. The emphasis is on quality and dependability.

The Market: Emulates New York's Grand Central Station and capitalises on the surging growth in fresh-food markets. The St Pancras Market sells the best fresh food from around London.

The Arcade: Takes its name from the brick arches, which house a range of boutiques. The focus here is on independent traders with high-quality products: Benugo, Le Pain Quotidien, Peyton & Byrne, Wilton and Noble, and Rituals, as well as some famous London shops such as Foyles the booksellers, and Hamleys the toyshop.

The Rendezvous: A new magnet for leisure-seeking Londoners. It includes Geronimo Inns' Betjeman Arms, Carluccio's and Europe's longest champagne bar and brasserie, operated by Searcy.

Above and below: The Circle at the north end of the public concourses provides larger retail units away from the hustle and bustle of the Arcade.

Station Art

The public enjoys art. London and Continental Stations and Property (LCSP) decided to bring art – sculpture, in particular – to St Pancras. Railway stations are important public spaces and LCSP felt they had a responsibility to create an interior public space that not only functioned efficiently, but which could also bring delight to the people who pass through the station. St Pancras had never been associated with art, but now, as part of its regeneration, it was decided to commission two major sculptures.

The Meeting Place

The brief was as concise as it was open-ended. The sculpture was to be called *The Meeting Place* and it was to represent the idea of 'meet me at St Pancras'. It was to be memorable and it was intended that it should become a monument that people would take to their hearts – as they had Alfred Gilbert's *Eros* in Piccadilly Circus or George Frampton's *Peter Pan* in Kensington Gardens. The piece was to be an extraordinary 9 metres (29 feet 6 inches) high so that it would not be lost in the vast train shed. And – appropriately enough, given its subject – it was to be situated beneath the great clock.

Paul Day was commissioned to undertake the work. He is well known for his Battle of Britain monument on the Embankment which was unveiled on 18 September 2005. With quite extraordinary daring, Day brings both perspective and movement into the monument. His work belongs, nevertheless, to the great European tradition of monumental sculpture. *The Meeting Place* shows two young lovers embracing. The young man has a rucksack and is, perhaps, a student. The young woman is casually, but smartly, dressed. He is English and she is French. St Pancras links England and France as never before. There are references – whether intentional or not, one cannot be sure – to that greatest of British romantic films, David Lean's *Brief Encounter* with Trevor Howard and the incomparable Celia Johnson. *The Meeting Place* will become a meeting place.

The Meeting Place embodies an *entente amicale* – he is English, she is French.

The arrival of *The Meeting Place* at St Pancras, 27 October 2007.

Paul Day's *The Meeting Place* under the clock, looking north.

Sir John Betjeman

Another sculpture, at platform level, pays tribute to Sir John Betjeman (1906–84). Poet Laureate from 1972 to 1984 – like Victorian laureate Alfred, Lord Tennyson – Betjeman was a great popular poet. More than anyone else he made people aware of the beauty of Victorian architecture through his colloquial eloquence. He did this at a time when the Modern Movement was triumphant and Victorian design was looked on with condescension. Betjeman probably did more than anyone else to transform the aesthetic sensibilities of the nation. It is largely to him that we owe the survival and subsequent revitalisation of St Pancras.

Holding on to his battered trilby, coat tails flapping, a shoe-lace undone and holding his Billingsgate Market bag of books, Betjeman looks up in wonder at one of the most beautiful and daring examples of nineteenth-century engineering. The bronze is by Martin Jennings, who read English at Oxford, later turning to sculpture. Despite its larger-than-life size, 2 metres (6 foot, 6 inches), people nevertheless empathise with the statue. From the day the station was opened it has proved immensely popular with the public.

Candida Lycett-Green, Betjeman's daughter, tells us: 'Whenever my father would visit either a tithe barn or awe-inspiring cathedral or railway station he would look up at the roof and whistle through his front teeth and say: "I say, this is a bit of alright."' Jennings captures that moment.

Fragments from some of Betjeman's poems are cut in an elegant italic into five Cumbrian black slate discs. These form an intriguing pathway to the statue. Like the poet, Jennings is fond of words.

John Betjeman arriving at a London Midland station; used on a poster for a play about the saving of St Pancras in June 2007.

Reading the poetry at Betjeman's feet.

Martin Jennings' statue of Sir John Betjeman,
spellbound in admiration of St Pancras station.

The small roundels contain the opening lines from some of his poems.

> A gentle guest, a willing host,
> Affection deeply planted –
> It's strange that those we miss the most
> Are those we take for granted.
> *The Hon. Sec.*

> Imprisoned in a cage of sound
> Even the trivial seems profound.
> *Uffington*

> Beyond the throb of the engines is the throbbing heart of all.
> *St Saviour's, Aberdeen Park, Highbury, London N1*

> Here where the cliffs alone prevail
> I stand exultant, neutral, free,
> And from the cushion of the gale
> Behold a huge consoling sea.
> *Winter Seascape*

> Revival ran along the hedge
> And made my spirit whole
> When steam was on the window panes
> And glory in my soul.
> *Undenominational*

A further quotation round the base of the statue captures a moment when Betjeman was gazing out to sea from the top of one of his beloved Cornish cliffs:

> And in the shadowless, unclouded glare
> Deep blue above us fades to whiteness where
> A misty sea-line meets the wash of air.
> *Cornish Cliffs*

And the roundel at the statue's feet reads:

> John Betjeman 1906–1984 Poet,
> Who saved this glorious station.

Chapter 12
The Royal Opening

The Royal Opening

On 6 November 2007, the actor Timothy West stood in the heart of St Pancras International, facing the royal party and more than 1,200 specially invited guests. He was playing the role of William Henry Barlow, the engineer for the Midland Railway who was responsible for the original station.

> 'Such a contrast with my feelings one chilly October morning in 1868 – the day we opened St Pancras for the first time. It is a day I remember, primarily for the absence of any celebration. We slipped on to the stage without a fanfare, without bunting or a brass band. Perhaps we were too exhausted – just get the station open and sell some tickets. After so much effort, so much heroic work – not to mark the opening was to say the very least, disappointing. But one hundred and thirty-nine years later – who would have thought it – the work will be celebrated and the moment marked with the dignity that such a glorious achievement merits.'

On that 'chilly October morning in 1868', St Pancras station slipped into the public consciousness with a whimper not an exaltation. Strange that such a majestic achievement, and one on such a heroic scale, should have been marked by an absence of celebration and pomp. After all, the St Pancras train shed was considered a true engineering wonder and was to be the largest single span enclosed space in the world for the next 24 years – a symbol of the power and ambition of Victorian Britain.

Even more importantly, St Pancras looked down on King's Cross station, with tracks rising 6 metres (19 feet 6 inches) higher but infinitely surpasssing it in style, luminescence and pure Gothic splendour. It held the high ground in every way possible.

The original opening of St Pancras station was an event of masterly understatement. Such a description could never be levelled against the dramatic, ambitious and stunning royal opening of St Pancras International. This was the day when St Pancras International was formally opened by the Her Majesty Queen Elizabeth II and His Royal Highness the Duke of Edinburgh. It was also the day that would signal to the world the completion of the Channel Tunnel Rail Link project – the new railway now called High Speed 1. Not only was this the day when the reborn St Pancras would at last be shown to the world; it was also the celebration of a new era in high-speed rail in the United Kingdom: a little more than two hours from the centre of London to the centre of Paris, with this incredible journey starting from a station that is as good as, if not better than, New York's legendary Grand Central.

And to all those cynics who questioned the expenditure of almost £6 billion on a high-speed railway to Paris and Brussels, the knowledge that St Pancras International and High Speed 1 were, in fact, acting as catalysts for the investment of over twice that amount in redevelopment for Kent and east London must have come as a revelation.

Actor Timothy West as William Barlow.

Pages 208–9: The Queen formally
opening St Pancras station and High
Speed 1, accompanied by Rob Holden.

From the very beginning, London & Continental Railways were convinced that the royal opening of St Pancras International had to match the scale and visual spectacle of the great station. After all, here was a good news story that should be screamed, shouted and yelled from the rooftops: a team of twenty-first-century entrepreneurs and engineers had not only dared to construct the first major railway for over a hundred years – and the UK's first real high-speed line – they had also delivered it 'on time and within budget'. On top of that, they had succeeded in doing what should have been done many years before: reversing the crime of neglect that had seen a national Grade I listed treasure wither and fade. They had made St Pancras train station beautiful once again.

The royal event was three years in the planning. The major challenge was to stage and deliver one of Europe's largest celebratory events, inside a fully-functioning train station that was just one week away from the beginning of

Her Majesty the Queen and HRH the Duke of Edinburgh greeted by the then Lord Lieutenant of Greater London, Lord Peter Imbert QPM JP, left, and Sir David Cooksey, chairman, second right, and Rob Holden, chief executive, far right, of London & Continental Railways board.

The Prime Minister, Gordon Brown, left, with Rob Holden and Stephen Jordan, managing director of LCSP, right.

Eurostar services. In the train shed, the station was being readied to send and receive the 400 metre (1,312 foot) long high-speed Eurostar train sets. Down below in the undercroft, Europe's newest destination station was being fitted out: the first Marks & Spencer in a railway station to sell food and clothes, boutique retail, cafés and bars – everything, in short, that would make St Pancras a destination in its own right, a place people would want to go to even if they weren't taking a train. The opening would take place inside the station: 1,200 people would be sitting on raked seating, looking down at the international platforms, as a full-scale concert orchestra trumpeted the entrance into the station of not just one, but three, high-speed trains. The station would be operational; the overhead catenary would be buzzing, and on the other side of the security screen it was necessary to present a passport. This was to be a royal opening on a grand scale, a night that none of the invited guests would forget.

The first sign that something very special was happening in the heart of London became apparent at about 6 pm when guests arrived in the Euston Road. St Pancras International was lit up like a beacon. Astronauts circling planet Earth could have sworn that north-west London had been specially illuminated to bring them safely home. The great Gothic towers of Sir George Gilbert Scott's façade were uplighted to perfection in shades of red, white and blue. Barlow's magnificent glazed roof was pulsating with radiant light.

BBC News helicopters were circling above, the reporters desperate to relay to the nation this unbelievable, once in a lifetime spectacle.

The VIP guests had arrived early and were in the undercroft, enjoying a champagne reception in a space that had been built 140 years earlier specifically to store Burton's beer barrels. There was not a bottle of beer in sight. The guests included the Prime Minister, Gordon Brown, and the Leader of the Opposition, David Cameron, as well as Ken Livingstone, John Prescott, Tessa Jowell, Boris Johnson and Lords Sebastian Coe and Michael Heseltine. As the time for the event drew nearer, the guests made their way up a grand staircase to the temporary seating overlooking the station platforms and the lights dimmed in expectation of what was to come.

Through the use of huge, moveable and divisible LCD screens suspended from the roof of Barlow's train shed, the guests were able to see the Queen and the Duke of Edinburgh arrive by car at the hotel arch beneath the Gothic façade of the Midland Grand Hotel, before they were greeted by Sir David Cooksey, chairman of London & Continental Railways. The royal party were led to a specially built dais under the great station clock and in front of the spectacular *Meeting Place* sculpture by Paul Day.

So far, the station had not been revealed in all its glory. Then the light show began, specially choreographed to a soundtrack played live in this railway cathedral by the Royal Philharmonic Concert Orchestra. These were musicians used to performing in the best venues around the world, yet you could see in their faces the joy and bewilderment of playing to the Queen in a restored train shed. In a station that was boldly rewriting the rules with twenty-first-century technology, the light show that revealed Barlow's train shed was almost embarrassingly breathtaking.

Out of the light and smoke walked William Henry Barlow, the Midland Railway's engineer for St Pancras, a leading civil engineer of his generation and a true scientific innovator. Played by the actor Timothy West, he welcomed

Above: The Royal Philharmonic Concert Orchestra, left, cameras and *The Meeting Place*, centre, and the invited audience, right, await the Queen's entrance onto the station concourse.

Below: The Queen and Rob Holden looking at *The Meeting Place*, the statue by sculptor Paul Day, right.

the royal party and assembled guests to his station. He talked about the 'Barlow boots' that helped carry the enormous weight of the train shed arches. He talked about the iconic roof, described by one wit at the time as 'a pair of lobster's claws'. And he marvelled at how he could now see through the platform into the undercroft – cutting the ties that bore the weight. 'And yet – the roof still stands.'

The impressive tracked LCD screens played a series of short films, starring David Coulthard, Kristin Scott Thomas and Terence Stamp, beautifully framing High Speed 1, Eurostar and, of course, St Pancras International.

Rob Holden, chief executive of London & Continental Railways then took to the stage to pay tribute to 'the people behind the project, the people who had the foresight to see the benefits of high-speed rail travel and the people, up to 9,000 of them, who have worked to successfully complete an infrastructure project that will be benefit millions of people today and for many decades to come'.

Her Majesty the Queen formally opened the station, talking about the very real benefits St Pancras and the high-speed line would bring to the nation.

Then came a unique moment: the arrival in the station of two Eurostar trains and one Hitachi Class 395 Javelin bullet train. This was the first time the bullet train had been seen in public – and the very first Japanese high-speed train to operate in Europe. The timing of this train cavalcade was choreographed perfectly with the orchestra and the hugely ambitious light show, which led gracefully into the Queen descending from her dais to meet the three drivers as they stood proudly by their trains.

The train cavalcade was greeted with great applause, the gleaming Hitachi bullet train reinforcing the fact that this was not just about international travel. In 2009, High Speed 1 will transform Kent's proximity to London with opportunities for new, fast domestic journeys; and in 2012, Javelin trains will speed spectators from St Pancras International to the Olympic Park in just seven minutes.

The train shed from the west side of the station during the offical royal opening. Her Majesty The Queen appears on the specially installed LCD screens. To the right is *The Meeting Place* and the Dent station clock, in the foreground the champagne bar awaits its first customers.

The Queen meets Alastair Lansley.

As the three trains powered down, the giant screens came alive with a dramatic short film that reminded guests that High Speed 1 is about more than a station and a railway; it is about the regeneration of north Kent, Stratford and King's Cross.

The royal party toured the undercroft, meeting representatives of the many staff who had contributed to the success of the works, and the Queen unveiled a plaque commemorating her visit and the completion of High Speed 1. Upstairs the entertainment continued around *The Meeting Place*.

In a modern spin on the historic and contemporary nature of the station, the worlds of opera and rhythm and blues collided perfectly as chart-topper Lemar joined opera diva Katherine Jenkins in a medley of Beatles' songs,

The Queen unveils a slate plaque commemorating the opening.

Ticket to Ride and *Hello/Goodbye*. The effect was heightened by the appearance of children from the Tower Hamlets New London Choir; the vibrancy of their voices and the sheer elation in their faces brought the proceedings to an emotional climax.

But it was William Henry Barlow who had the last word:

> St Pancras – this great railway station – no longer full of smoke and grime, but light, air and music. Not just a place to hurry through on your way to somewhere better. It is now somewhere to arrive – a place for that special rendezvous. Time to let the twenty-first century move on.

Two Eurostars and a Hitachi unit inaugurate a new era at St Pancras accompanied by a sound and light show.

1844

10 May: The Midland Railway founded at a meeting held at the Sun Inn, Eastwood, Nottinghamshire. It incorporated the North Midland, Midland Counties and Birmingham Junction Railways whose lines converged at Derby.

George Hudson
Courtesy of the Institution of Civil Engineers

The brilliantly entrepreneurial George Hudson (1800–71) – the earliest 'railway king' – was the Midland Railway's first chairman but his dubious accounting practices led to his downfall in 1849.

William Henry Barlow (1812–1902) joins the Midland Railway.

Sir William Henry Barlow
Courtesy of the Institution of Civil Engineers

1846

27 June: Metropolitan Railway termini commissioners report on the location of central London stations and schemes within or in the immediate vicinity of the metropolis.

1847

George Gilbert Scott visits Belgium en route to Germany to study German Gothic before beginning work on the competition for the Nikolaikirche in Hamburg. He wins the competition. He is particularly impressed with the immense medieval Cloth Hall in Ypres. Certain features of this appear in his 1865 design for the Midland Grand Hotel.

1849

John Ellis (1789–1862) succeeds George Hudson as chairman of the Midland Railway after Hudson's exposure. The Midland Railway is in a weak financial position and its dividends have fallen from 6 per cent in 1844 to 3 per cent.

1850

24 February: St Luke's temporary church, King's Cross (located on site of Small Pox Hospital) opens for divine services.

Great Northern temporary terminus opens at Maiden Lane (now York Way).

1851

30 March: St Luke's temporary church, King's Cross, dismantled and re-erected later on Euston Road.

1852

14 October: King's Cross station opens.

1853

James Joseph Allport (1811–92) becomes manager of the Midland Railway. With a three-year gap between 1857 and 1860 (during which he managed a shipyard in Jarrow) he remains with the Midland for 31 years.

Sir James Allport
Courtesy of the Institution of Civil Engineers

14 October: King's Cross station opens. Architect: Lewis Cubitt (1799–1883).

The Government orders St Pancras vestry not to bury any more bodies in its churchyard.

1854

17 May: The Great Northern Hotel opens.

December: Baxter House, St Pancras, Sir Henry Bessemer undertakes a series of small-scale and purely empirical experiments that lead indirectly to the development of mild steel and the first rolling of steel rails at Dowlais in 1856. He built a works at Baxter House in the 'quiet suburb of St Pancras', on a site in St Pancras Lane, later covered by the Midland Railway coal drops. He was extremely secretive about the process, building a wall separating the engine and boiler house from the machinery; even his sons were not allowed in until they were grown up.

1856

2 July: St Luke's Church (architect: John Johnson (1807–78)) foundation stone laid on what was to be site of St Pancras station.

1857

8 May: The Midland Railway extension to Hitchin, Hertfordshire, is opened. This brings the Midland Railway metals within striking distance of London. The Great Northern Railway now provides a conditional route for the Midland Railway to access London, north of King's Cross.

12 May: End of 'Common Purpose' Agreement between London & North Western Railway and Midland Railway.

Barlow sets up in private practice as a consulting engineer. As a consultant, he remains closely associated with the Midland Railway throughout the remainder of his career.

George Gilbert Scott publishes *Remarks on Secular & Domestic Architecture Present & Future* in which he advocates Gothic as an appropriate style for the industrial age. He praises some railway architecture.

1858

1 February: The Midland Railway starts running some of its trains into a station north of the Regent's Canal and King's Cross rather than Euston.

The clearance of some of Agar Town is authorised for the erection of the Midland Railway's coal depot.

The Fleet River is encased in a tunnel and becomes part of the London sewerage system.

1859

Work begins on the Metropolitan Railway from Paddington to Farringdon, the world's first underground railway: this causes the Great Northern Hospital (thought to be the Fever Hospital on the site of the Great Northern Hotel) to be moved.

1860

The Imperial Gas Company buys out some of the lessees in Agar Town cheaply and erects two groups of two (doublet) telescopic gas holders there.

1861

30 May: St Luke's Church consecrated.

The German Gymnastics Society is formed and a Turnhalle (gymnasium) is commissioned.

1862

9 May: First Bessemer steel rail laid at Camden goods station.

Sir Henry Bessemer vacates Baxter House to make way for Midland Railway goods depot. His steel-making enterprise moves to Sheffield.

1863

10 January: Metropolitan Railway passenger services begin between Edgware Road and King's Cross. This is the world's first underground railway.

22 June: Royal Assent given to the Bedford to St Pancras Railway Act.

1 October: Metropolitan Railway connection opened into Great Northern Railway network. Tunnelling work uses the 'cut and cover' method. A wide trench was dug, with brick side walls to support the soil. Once the track was laid, the cutting was roofed over with brickwork and the ground surface restored.

1864

January: Barlow sets out an ambitious four-year timetable for the completion of the line to St Pancras in a letter to the Midland Railway Board after negotiations with the Great Northern Railway for a new joint line to London break down.

St Pancras Ironwork Co. is established in Pancras Road.

Above: St Pancras Ironwork Co. grating in Grand Place, Brussels and, left, on the clock tower at The Angel, Islington. The name of the horse was Ever Ran
Courtesy of Bernard Gambrill

1865

2 January: Opening of Midland Railway's first 'railway' property in London. This site was always called St Pancras goods depot although it was properly located in Agar Town, farther north.

The Midland Railway board invites a number of architects to submit designs for a large station hotel as frontage to Barlow and Ordish's train shed. Among the competing architects were Edward Middleton Barry (1830–80), George Somers Clarke (1825–82), Owen Jones (1809–74), George Gilbert Scott (1811–78) and Thomas Charles Sorby (1836–1924).

The construction of a group of three telescopic gas holders (the triplet gas holder group) is completed at the corner of Wharf Road and Old St Pancras Road (now Goods Way and Pancras Road).

The German Gymnasium (Edward Grüning (1837–1908)) is completed in Pancras Road; it is the earliest surviving purpose-built public gymnasium in the country.

1869 The German Gymnasium: Ladies' Class
Illustrated London News, Courtesy of Camden Local Studies & Archives Centre

Ernest Ravenstein (1834–1913), one of the directors of the German Gymnastics Society, organises the National Olympian Games in London for following year.

The erection of the five blocks of Stanley Buildings by the Improved Industrial Dwelling Company is completed.

Eleven entries are submitted in the competition to design the hotel that the Midland Railway plans to build at St Pancras station. George Gilbert Scott wins.

1866

1 January: King's Cross (York Way) station platform opens on Metropolitan Railway connection.

The designs for the Midland Grand Hotel submitted by George Gilbert Scott (1811–78, knighted in 1872) are accepted after revisions are made to the originals (a reduction in scope by the loss of one storey).

The indoor events of the National Olympian Games are held at the new German Gymnasium in Pancras Road, the outdoor events are held on the River Thames and at Crystal Palace. W. G. Grace, at the age of only eighteen, wins the 440-yard hurdles at these Games. He goes on to become the one of the most famous cricketers in history.

The Midland Railway obtains parliamentary consent to demolish the remaining houses in Agar Town and build the railway line into St Pancras station over the land. Three thousand properties are said to have been pulled down.

St Pancras is the most densely populated part of the London metropolis.

Metropolitan Line excavation beneath what is now the Midland Grand Hotel forecourt
© *NRM/Science & Society Picture Library*

The Fleet sewer at the junction of Midland Road and Goods Way
Both from Frederick Smeeton Williams, The Midland Railway: Its Rise and Progress, *David & Charles, first published in 1877*

Bodies in St Pancras churchyard that were accidentally disinterred by the construction of Midland Railways' line into St Pancras station are reburied, not for the last time; macabre stories had been reported of workers playing football with skulls. Thomas Hardy (1840–1928), as a trainee architect, oversees the removal of the bodies.

1867

St Luke's Church is dismantled to make way for St Pancras station, and the materials carted to be re-erected on corner of Grosvenor Road and Nightingale Lane, Wanstead, Essex. It is now a United Reformed Church. The Midland Railway has to pay for the construction of a replacement church, St Luke's at Oseney Crescent, New Kentish Town.

November: First section of St Pancras wrought-iron roof truss erected by the Butterley Company of Derby. The brickwork and the foundations are by Waring Brothers. Barlow's and Ordish's train shed is the largest single span enclosed space until it is surpassed by Dutert's and Contamin's Palais des Machines at the Exposition Universelle, Paris, 1889 (demolished 1909). St Pancras is the largest surviving nineteenth-century enclosed space.

Erection of first train shed trussed arch
© *NRM/Science & Society Picture Library*

St Pancras water point is erected to refill engines for their next duty.

1868

13 July: Midland Railway train services start from Bedford to Moorgate using Midland Railways' Metropolitan branch tunnel.

30 September: Waring Brothers' dinner to celebrate the opening of the New Midland Terminus is held at the Great Northern Hotel.

1 October, 4.20 am: The first train arrives at St Pancras – the 10.05 pm overnight mail from Leeds.

The Midland Railway stops using the Great Northern route into the King's Cross area.

1869

Spring: St Pancras station completed.

The western booking hall at St Pancras station is completed; the block of offices built to the north of it is eventually named Barlow House.

Construction of the Midland Grand Hotel begins.

Midland Railway Cresting
Courtesy of the Midland Railway Society

1870

Two extra tracks are laid from St Pancras goods yard into St Pancras causing further disturbance to St Pancras graveyard.

29 March: Barlow describes the construction of the St Pancras train shed roof in detail before the Institution of Civil Engineers, 'For the details of the roof I am indebted to Mr Ordish, whose practical knowledge and excellent suggestions enabled me, while adhering to the form, depth and general design, to effect many Improvements in its construction.'

1873

5 May: The east wing of the Midland Grand Hotel (more than 300 rooms) opens to the public.

Samuel Waite Johnson (1831–1912) is appointed as Locomotive Superintendent of the Midland Railway. His locomotives are considered to have been among the most perfect – aesthetically and functionally – of the nineteenth century.

Samuel Waite Johnson, Midland Locomotive Superintendent 1872–1903

1874

An application by the Midland Railway for the demolition of St Pancras Old Church and churchyard is refused. The approaches to St Pancras are split on two separate viaducts. These divide the graveyard into three portions.

The first Pullman Train in the UK operates on Midland Railway.

The Midland Railway acquires the site where the British Library stands today for the Somers Town goods depot: the application to build is granted resulting in the demolition of the 4,000 homes and the displacement of 10,000 people. The Midland Railway is forced to provide alternative housing.

18 December: King's Cross local station opens.

1876

The west wing of the Midland Grand Hotel is completed and George Gilbert Scott is finally paid off, eight years after construction started. The total building cost is £438,000.

1878

1 February: King's Cross suburban station opened, extended in 1880 and rebuilt in 1895.

1880

James Joseph Allport (1811–92) resigns as manager of the Midland Railway and is elected to the board of directors. His greatest achievements are to bring the Midland Railway to London and the creation of St Pancras station and the Midland Grand Hotel. He is knighted in 1884.

1883

Work starts on the construction of the Somers Town goods Depot, delayed by rehousing those displaced.

1884

Second tunnel at Belsize (Park) opened to alleviate congestion caused by interlaced tracks through the original tunnel.

1885

13 March: Brewer and Skinner Streets renamed Midland Road.

1887

Somers Town goods depot is completed.

1892

The construction of Culross Buildings as homes for railway servants is completed by the Great Northern Railway; they take their name from Charles Colville (Lord Culross), Chairman of the Great Northern Railway 1872–95.

25 April: Death of Sir James Allport in the Midland Grand Hotel.

St Pancras train shed c.1890
Mary Evans Picture Library

Going North? St Pancras
Midland Railway poster 1910 by Fred Taylor
Mary Evans Picture Library

1902

12 November: William Henry Barlow dies in Charlton, Greenwich.

1904

The St Pancras Works stops manufacturing gas.

1907

The German Gymnasium closes.

1914

4 August: The First World War begins.

1917

17–18 February: The German Gymnasium and St Pancras station are both damaged in a bomber raid and an air attack is made on the Somers Town goods yard. The Gotha aircraft used in the attacks was the first long-range bomber.

By 1917, Midland traffic is reduced to 50 per cent of its pre-war mileage.

Midland Railway Wyvern Crest 1844–1922
© Historical Model Railway Society 1975

1923

After the war, the railways are not permitted by the Government to return to their pre-war competitive positions. Under the stipulations of the Railways Act 1921, the 120 separate British railway undertakings are reorganised to become four large groupings: London, North Eastern Railway (LNER), London, Midland and Scottish (LMS), Southern Railway (SR) and Great Western Railway (GWR). Midland Railway – probably the strongest of the pre-war railways – is incorporated into the LMS. The livery of the Midland Railway becomes the livery of the LMS.

London Midland & Scottish Railway emblem 1923–47
Courtesy of Iain Logan

1924

15 December: King's Cross local station extension opens.

1935

19 April: The Midland Grand Hotel closes due to poor profits; it is converted into offices for the London, Midland & Scottish Railway and renamed St Pancras Chambers.

1939

3 September: The Second World War begins.

1940

11 May: King's Cross station is bombed.

16 October: Underground tunnels between King's Cross and Farringdon bombed: a 1-tonne bomb closes lines; 14 people killed.

1941

March: Underground services between King's Cross and Farringdon resume.

9–10 March: The platforms and roof at King's Cross station are badly damaged by a bomb: two die and three people are injured.

1942

17 August: St Pancras bombed. A 500kg bomb penetrates the train shed roof and causes severe damage to platforms 3 and 4. The bomb also damages the vaults below and the Metropolitan Underground line. Remarkably, St Pancras is back in service after a week of emergency repairs.

7 August 1942: St Pancras bomb damage
© Hulton Getty/Science & Society Picture Library

1946

Plans are proposed to demolish and rebuild King's Cross station: nothing comes of them.

1947

St Pancras 'Throat' (approach tracks) remodelled.

1948

1 January: British railways are nationalised under the British Transport Commission.

BR logotype 1948–56
Heraldic Devices held by Garter King of Arms

1952

In his survey *The Buildings of England: London*, Nikolaus Pevsner praises Barlow and Ordish's train shed as a model of Victorian functionalism. He is more cautious about Scott's.

Midland Grand Hotel: 'No London hotel … was … quite so splendid and varied in appearance … on the principle of free grouping so dear to present-day architects …The carriage ramp up to the drive-in should also delight the eye of the modern designer.'

Sir Nikolaus Pevsner (1902–83), founder chairman of the Victorian Society
UPP/Topfoto

1957

Interior of train shed and booking hall woodwork cleaned and restored.

1958–59

The glazed area of the train shed roof is enlarged to provide additional natural light on the concourse.

British Railways totem sign
Courtesy of BRB Residuary Ltd

1959

The British Transport Commission proposes to rebuild Euston station, which entails demolishing the Great Hall and the Doric Arch.

St Pancras refreshment facilities opened.

1960

4 July: Midland Blue Pullman (Class 251) weekday service between Manchester Central (Now G-Mex) and St Pancras commences.

1960 Midland Region Blue Pullman Unit (Class 251)
© NRM/Science & Society Picture Library

1960s

The Midland Railway's coal drops in Camley Street are demolished; the area becomes a municipal rubbish tip.

BR logotype 1956–65 on London Midland Region Crimson Lake
Heraldic Devices held by Garter King of Arms

1961

St Pancras Cruising Club founded at St Pancras Basin.

1962

Phillip Hardwick's Doric Propylaeum – the Euston Arch, the grand monumental entry to Euston station – is demolished on the orders of the British Railways Board. The destruction of a much-loved landmark arouses great controversy. John Betjeman leads the protests. The conservation movement learns tactical skills from this defeat.

The Euston Arch 1837–1962
Courtesy of Bernard Gambrill

1963

A 73 m- (240 ft-) long glazed barrier with train indicators is erected behind buffer stops.

1 July: Beer traffic into the undercroft ceases.

John Betjeman at Broad Street station, 1971
Photographed by Lord Snowdon / Camera Press

1966

The British Railways Board proposes to 'combine' (demolish) both King's Cross and St Pancras stations: permission is denied.

19 December: The Somers Town goods depot is designated by the government as the site of the new British Library.

BR logotype 1965–97
Corporate Identity by the BRB Design Panel under chairmanship of Milner Gray © British Railways Board

1967

March: Midland Blue Pullman service ceases (after the opening of London Euston to Manchester Piccadilly electrification scheme) and units are transferred to Western Region.

2 November: St Pancras station and Chambers are listed as Grade 1 by English Heritage.

1968

December: St Pancras closure plan scrapped.

1973

3 June: King's Cross concourse and travel centre opened with temporary planning permission.

1976

May: Last Anglo-Scottish train services run from St Pancras.

Wayland Young, Lord Kennet 1966–70 Parliamentary Secretary (Junior Minister), Ministry of Housing & Local Government
Courtesy of Lord Kennet

1977

Bernard Kaukas appointed BR Director Environment. BRB authorises £440,000 contract for St Pancras cleaning and restoration.

4 March: King's Cross suburban and York Road platforms closed.

1978

Five-year programme of cleansing and restoration commences.

Application for replacement of St Pancras booking office by BR to designs of Manning, Clamp & Partners, consulting architects.

1980

January: St Pancras cleansing work halted after completion of west tower and wing and part of Midland Road elevation.

1980–83

Train shed interior cleaned and 122 roof floodlights installed.

August: BR appeal against decision by London Borough of Camden to refuse permission for replacement of the booking office. The appeal fails.

Bernard Kaukas, BRB Chief Architect 1968 and Director Environment 1977
Courtesy of Bernard Kaukas

1982

4 October: Introduction of high-speed Inter-City (Class 253) services to Nottingham and Sheffield.

1983

28 March: First electric trains run into St Pancras.

May: Refurbished booking office opens with ticket office repositioned on western wall.

St Pancras to Bedford electrification scheme commences operation after two-year train manning dispute.

Final railway staff (Travellers Fare) leave St Pancras Chambers; Scott's building now stands empty.

1984

28 March: Full electric services commence after train modifications, two years late.

1986

Four of the gas holders on the railway lands are listed (Grade II).

1987

February: The Channel Tunnel Act receives Royal Assent, and Waterloo is named the first terminal for international services. Waterloo is chosen as the site for the first terminal for the international passenger services through the Channel Tunnel.

July: British Rail (BR) begins a study of long-term capacity needed for Channel Tunnel services, King's Cross is chosen as a second station. Without a new route 45 million passenger journeys before 2040 would be compromised and road congestion would impose enormous social and environmental costs. One hundred sites are investigated. Environmental consultants are appointed to investigate the preferred route options.

House of Lords Select Committee announces that King's Cross station is the ideal site for the terminus of the Channel Tunnel Rail Link (CTRL).

1988

January: BR identifies four possible routes for CTRL.

The number of potential developers of the King's Cross Railway lands is reduced to Speyhawk/McAlpine and London Regeneration Consortium (LRC), a partnership between the National Freight Corporation and Rosehaugh Stanhope.

The Victorian Society publishes *Opportunity or Calamity: the King's Cross Railway Lands Development.*

English Heritage publishes an inventory of the architectural and industrial features that are considered important within the King's Cross Railway lands.

2 June: British Railways Board (BRB) chooses the LRC to become the development partners of the 135 acres of derelict railway lands at King's Cross; LRC declare that Foster Associates are the chosen master-planners.

July: BRB publishes 'Channel Tunnel Services: A Study of Long Term Terminal and Route Option Capacity'. This describes four viable routes across Kent, which are identified by the engineers and environmental consultants. The design team suffers from a lack of understanding of the real impacts of a new railway. The uncertainty causes widespread blight and anxiety.

July 1988 BRB Study of Terminals and Routes
Courtesy of BRB Residuary Ltd

November: British Rail's private Bill authorising the construction of the Channel Tunnel Rail Link terminal at King's Cross is deposited in Parliament.

282 petitions received against British Rail's private King's Cross Railways Bill for the construction of the CTRL terminal at King's Cross are lodged in Parliament.

1989

January: The Rail Link Project team formed in Croydon. BR starts house purchases to reduce hardship for people unable to sell their property in the route corridors. BR appoints four engineering consultancies to examine different route sections and to define engineering standards.

March: First single route option announced publicly to reduce uncertainty. The route is an amalgam of those previously announced.

May: A planning application is submitted for a new enclosed concourse between King's Cross and St Pancras stations involving the demolition of the Great Northern Hotel.

June: The Parliamentary Select Committee on British Rail's King's Cross Railways Bill begins sitting: evidence is heard for 13 days before the recess.

July: Public consultation for the rail link begins with a view to the submission of a parliamentary Bill in November. A private Bill is in preparation.

3 November: BR's Channel Tunnel team is set up. British Railways Board announces a joint venture with Eurorail comprising Trafalgar House & British Insulated Callenders Cables (BICC) to take the CTRL project forward.

The proposed Channel Tunnel Rail Link Bill is modified to provide a new line only between Cheriton and Swanley but this Bill is eventually abandoned.

Eurorail Logotype 1989–91

December: The King's Cross Railways Bill select committee resumes.

1990

The BR/Trafalgar House & BICC joint venture task force works to improve the proposals by making them better value for money as well as to reduce the impact of construction.

The King's Cross Railways Bill select committee continues to sit (for a total of 51 days' hearings, it is among the longest private Bill hearings to date).

The office and residential property market collapses.

Foster Associates scheme for the Railway lands is discarded.

June: Secretary of State Cecil Parkinson rejects the BRB/Trafalgar House & BICC proposals. The route between the Channel Tunnel and the River Medway is accepted and safeguarded. He widens the brief to the project team by asking the joint venture to evaluate routes from Medway to central London in more detail, improve the benefits to domestic and international passengers, as well as develop a freight strategy and evaluate routes proposed by other people.

The proponents of the other routes, London Borough of Newham, Rail Europe and Ove Arup, are commissioned to work up their proposals so that a valid comparison can be made with the BR proposals.

July: British Railways King's Cross Railways Bill is approved by the House of Commons and passed to the House of Lords.

December: *The People's Brief* is prepared by independent planning consultant, Mike Parkes, in conjunction with King's Cross Railway Lands Group (KXRLG): it suggests that St Pancras station is a far more logical terminus site for the CTRL than King's Cross.

Channel connection

BR Channel connection logotype
Courtesy of BRB Residuary Ltd

1991

May: BRB submits a southerly route for the CTRL to the Department of Transport to be considered along with options proposed by the other organisations who advocate an eastern approach. The BR publication, 'Comparison of Routes', is sent to the Government.

Rosehaugh and Stanhope declare financial problems and sell off some assets to reduce borrowing.

14 October: The Government formally announces its decision to Parliament that an eastern approach route is to be adopted for the CTRL. The Government says that its choice is determined by its potential regeneration benefits.

November: The Rail Link Project is reorganised to accommodate new objectives and now operates as agents for the Department of Transport.

December: The Department of Transport forms a team to look into the benefits of Public Private Partnerships: the team includes Samuel Montague, WS Atkins and the Bank of England. (This team reported its conclusions in 1993.)

European Passenger Services monogram
Courtesy of LCR

1992

13 January: Commons debate on Amendments to Provisions of the King's Cross Railways Bill.

5 May: BR announces a £7M contract for the two-year programme of external restoration for St Pancras.

May: King's Cross Railway Lands Group publishes an *Environmental Impact Statement* to support the two alternative planning applications that it has submitted for the development of the Railway lands.

28 July: BR's project team forms Union Railways as a BR agency company comprising public and private sector staff. BR technical experts work with six private-sector engineering consultancies and 11 environmental consultants working on 14 disciplines, including aquatics, community, ecology, landscape, noise and waste management, to prepare an environmental appraisal for the project.

Rosehaugh ceases trading, insolvent.

1993

Scott's Midland Grand Hotel now stands empty.

29 January: London Underground (King's Cross) Act 1995 (1993c.i) 'An Act to empower London Underground Limited, for safety purposes and the relief of passenger congestion, to construct works and to acquire or use lands; to confer further powers on the Company, and for connected purposes.'

Union Railways appointed to oversee the CTRL project, announces initial plans for its construction; 1.5 million hours have been expended on developing an acceptable route and £2 million have been spent on investigating environmental impacts.

22 March: John McGregor, the Secretary of State, makes a statement on the Government's preferred alignment of the CTRL. The consultation would follow a single route from Channel Tunnel to Barking, where two options would be considered into King's Cross and St Pancras stations.

17 May: Eurostar international terminal (architect: Nicholas Grimshaw with YRM) opens at Waterloo; the services are delayed for a year because the Channel Tunnel is not ready for operation until May 1994.

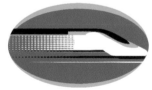

Union Railways logotype, 1998
Courtesy of Union Railways

1994

24 January: The Government reaffirms its preference for the eastern approach route, naming St Pancras as the London terminus.

February: The competition to appoint a private sector promoter to design, build, finance and operate the CTRL is launched.

6 May: HM Queen Elizabeth II opens the Channel Tunnel.

9 June: From the nine bidding consortia that have applied for pre-qualification as constructors, maintainers and operators of the CTRL, four are selected to submit full proposals: Green Arrow, Eurorail, London & Continental Railways (LCR) and Union Link.

August: The Government announces plans for a new CTRL station at Ebbsfleet in north Kent.

14 November: First Eurostar train service starts from Waterloo.

November: The hybrid Channel Tunnel Rail Link Bill is deposited in Parliament.

Union Railways colophon
Courtesy of Union Railways

1995

994 individuals, businesses and other organisations petition Parliament against the Channel Tunnel Rail Link Bill.

April: Union Railways Limited (URL) and European Passenger Services Limited (EPSL, later Eurostar UK Ltd) are transferred from the BRB to the Department of Transport in preparation for privatisation after the selection of a promoter.

June: From the four full proposals submitted by the selected consortia and adjudicated by the Department for Transport and its advisers, London & Continental Railways and Eurorail are shortlisted to enter the final stage of the competition.

THE DEPARTMENT OF TRANSPORT

1996
29 February: LCR is awarded the CTRL contract.

29 February 1996: Sir George Young MP, Secretary of Transport with John Watts MP, Parliamentary Minister for Railways at the anouncement of the appointment of London & Continental Railways as promoter of the Channel Tunnel Rail Link. *Courtesy of Union Railways*

May: Formal transfer of the project to LCR, including Union Railways and European Passenger Services Ltd. With the appointment of LCR comes the decision to include the station at Stratford, which is to be a key part of its commercial strategy.

3 October: Lord Ampthill, Chair of the House of Lords' Select Committee on the Channel Tunnel Rail Link Bill, says, 'The people of Camden must be prepared to put up with hell for the next few years for the sake of this project.'

18 December: Channel Tunnel Rail Link Bill receives Royal Assent.

1997
January: LCR applies for powers under the Transport and Works Act 1992 to construct Stratford International station and a twin-track connection to the West Coast Main Line outside St Pancras for direct connections to the north.

LCR plans to raise the necessary private-sector finance through bank financing and equity raising through a stock-market flotation.

Eurostar logotype 1994
Courtesy of Eurostar UK

1994 Department of Transport logotype
© Department for Transport

1998
January: Eurostar revenues are not as great as forecast by LCR in its bid, or indeed by any other party connected with the bid. As a result, there is growing concern that LCR's traffic projections and consequent revenue stream are unrealistic. LCR is unable to implement its original financing plan for the project and seeks an additional £1.2 billion of public-sector support to achieve a financing of the project. The Deputy Prime Minister refuses to agree to this request and directs LCR to find risk-sharing partners.

28 January: John Prescott, the Deputy Prime Minister announces to the House of Commons that LCR is unable to raise the finance for the CTRL.

LCR Logotype 1994
London & Continental Railways

3 June: Announcement in both Houses of Parliament that LCR's revised proposal involving Railtrack is acceptable to the Government. The new arrangements do not require any significant increase in public-sector support in present value terms. Railtrack underwrites the construction of Section 1 which it will acquire on completion, and has an option to do the same for Section 2. In recognition of the unique features of the project and of the Government's continuing commitment, £3.75 billion of privately raised debt is Government-guaranteed to reduce the overall cost of financing and extend the period over which it needs to be repaid.

LCR appoints a consortium of National Express, SNCF (the National Railway of France), SNCB (the National Railway of Belgium) and British Airways to manage the Eurostar (UK) business. The contract will run until 2010. The CTRL concession is shortened to 2086 and Eurostar operation will return to Government ownership in 2086.

Decision announced that the CTRL is to be constructed in two sections: Section 1 from the Channel Tunnel to Fawkham Junction, via Southfleet in Kent; Section 2 from Southfleet to St Pancras through Stratford.

15 October: Deputy Prime Minister John Prescott MP attends the groundbreaking ceremony on the west bank of the River Medway to start work on Section 1.

LCE logotype 1994–97
Courtesy of Rail Link Engineering

RLE logotype 1994–97
Courtesy of Rail Link Engineering

2001
February: The Great Northern Hotel closes.

March: The Transport & Works Act Order for Stratford station and the West Coast Main Line (WCML) link is confirmed.

3 April: Railtrack is in financial difficulties. It relinquishes its option to take forward Section 2 as it does not have the financial capacity to undertake the project. The Government approves LCR's alternative proposals to take forward Section 2 under a Cost Overrun Protection Programme (COPP) developed and arranged by one of its founder shareholders, Bechtel. Under the COPP, Bechtel, RLE and the insurance market take on two-thirds of the risk of cost overruns in the areas of risk covered by the Programme.

3 April 2001: Bernard Gambrill, John Prescott MP and Frank Dobson MP checking the St Pancras model. Government approves the proposals for taking forward CTRL Section 2.
Courtesy of Union Railways

21 July: Construction begins on Section 2 and Minister for Transport, John Spellar MP, attends the groundbreaking ceremony at Stratford.

8 October: Railtrack goes into Railway Administration.

9 December: Last steam train enters St Pancras train shed.

9 December 2001: the last steam engine in St Pancras
Duchess of Sutherland **Princess Royal Class locomotive**
No 4233. © *Chris Milner*

2002

Graves displaced in the original St Pancras cemetery are uncovered and reburied at Finchley during the construction of the station extension.

3 October: Railtrack ownership of the domestic railway network is taken over by Network Rail.

LCR agrees terms with Railtrack Group to purchase its interest in Section 1 of the Link. The department evaluates the deal and approves it.

2003

30 July: Official test run on the track of Section 1. A Eurostar train breaks the UK rail-speed record with a speed of 334.7 km/h, beating the previous UK record of 259.5 km/h set in 1979 by the BR Advanced Passenger Train.

16 September: The Prime Minister formally accepts completion of Section 1, 'on time' and 'on budget'.

28 September: commercial Eurostar services commence over Section 1.

Section 1 opening day logotype
Courtesy of Eurostar UK

28 September: Section 2 is approximately 50 per cent complete.

18 December: Union Railways applies for planning permission from Camden Council to work 24 hours a day, 7 days a week, on the Thameslink station 'box' beneath Midland Road:

Camden Council, Coopers Lane Residents Association, KXRLG and many others call for a public enquiry into the planning application.

2004

27 January: Secretary of State for Transport, Alistair Darling, attends the 'break-through' ceremony north of St Pancras as the first tunnel-boring machine completes its drive from Stratford.

January: The public enquiry into Union Railways' planning application to work 24 hours a day, 7 days a week, on the Thameslink station works opens; it is scheduled to last for two days but it is extended to five.

11 February: Planning Inspector announces the result of the public enquiry: the extended hours application for the Thameslink 'box' is turned down; the temporary closure of Thameslink is extended by 10 weeks as a result.

23 March: Completion of the London tunnels.

9 April: The Barlow train shed at St Pancras closes for renovation after the last Midland Mainline departure.

12 April: Midland Mainline services start to operate from a temporary home on the eastern half of the new St Pancras extension.

St Pancras International logotype
London & Continental Railways

June: Outline planning consent obtained for Stratford City development and application made for consent at King's Cross Central.

11 September: Cross-London Thameslink services are suspended for six months to allow construction of the new Thameslink station 'box' beneath Midland Road.

2005

17 February: The International Olympic Committee's evaluation team for the 2012 Games is driven from Stratford to St Pancras through the CTRL tunnels to demonstrate the potential of the proposed Olympic shuttle.

16 May: Cross-London Thameslink services resume following completion, on time, of the Midland Road box.

2006

8 February: Government gives the go-ahead for the fit-out of the Thameslink box station.

17 July: The western half of the St Pancras extension is completed on time, and Midland Mainline moves to its permanent home at platforms 1 to 4.

14 November: CTRL is renamed High Speed 1, and the

opening date for Section 2 announced: one year to go.

2007

7 January: The overhead power lines on Section 2 go live at 25,000 volts.

6 March: The first Eurostar enters St Pancras on test.

First Eurostar enters St Pancras station
© *Eddie MacDonald*

16 March: Archbishop Richard Arthur Dillon (died in 1806), an exile from the French Revolution, is re-interred in Narbonne, France after the exhumation of the coffin in St Pancras churchyard.

12 June: The International Olympic Committee, evaluating London's progress towards 2012 is carried by Eurostar train from Stratford to St Pancras in less than seven minutes, demonstrating the potential of the Olympic Javelin shuttle.

6 November: Official royal opening of St Pancras International by HM Queen Elizabeth II.

14 November: Section 2 opens; High Speed 1 becomes operational. Eurostar switches its operation from Waterloo International to St Pancras International.

9 December: Thameslink station opens below new St Pancras.

High Speed Line 1 logotype
London & Continental Railways

Experience the Incredible Journey!
This document, compiled by Bernard Gambrill, is an amalgam of other chronologies produced by the King's Cross Railway Lands Group, Department for Transport, The Channel Tunnel Rail Link, The Bartlett Faculty of the Built Environment, Stuart Durant, Alan A. Jackson's 'London Terminus', revised 1986 and project diaries.

Their assistance is gratefully acknowledged.

Commissioned from the artist Peter Green, *Allegory: The Spirits of St Pancras* shows the trains and locomotives that have used St Pancras station from the arrival of the first train at 4 am on 1 October 1868 until the opening of St Pancras International on 14 November 2007. The trains are described from left to right.

A Midland Railway brake and luggage carriage, a contemporary of the Johnson locomotive on its right. The advanced design of Midland's carriages incorporated a sophisticated braking system.

A 4-2-2 'Spinner', designed by the Midland Railway's Samuel Waite Johnson, and introduced in 1887. Johnson's locomotives were elegant and with their very large single driving wheels they were also fast and efficient. On heavy trains the Midland was obliged to use two locomotives.

A Eurostar service departing for the Continent. Its length is accommodated by a new extension to the great St Pancras train shed of 1868. The design is derivative of the French TGV (*train à grand vitesse*), which revolutionised rail travel in France. The TGV's principal designer was French-based Briton Jack Cooper who had worked with American designer Raymond Loewy, a champion of streamlined form. The nose of the Eurostar's power car is closer to that of the British high-speed train than to Cooper's original TGV design. In its styling, it is a true derivative of the British high-speed train as it was designed by British designers Jones Garrard, founded by Roger Jones, one of the original designers of the British Rail high-speed train power car. Michael Rodber, another director, completed the styling. Eurostar trains have a maximum speed of 300 km/h (186 mph).

An InterCity 125 — introduced in 1976. Two diesel engines provide 1.7 megawatts (2,250 HP) have made possible regular speeds of up to 200 km/h (124 mph).

A 4-6-0 'Jubilee' class engine, designed by William Stanier (1876–1965), London, Midland & Scottish Railway's chief mechanical engineer. This steam locomotive was introduced in 1934 and 191 were built. The coaches are in the crimson and cream livery adopted by British Railways for locomotive-hauled rolling stock soon after nationalisation in 1948. Stanier was a Fellow of the Royal Society and knighted in 1943.

The Class 45 or 'Peak' is a powerful diesel-electric locomotive of 1.9 megawatts (2,500 HP) which first saw service in the early 1960s. Peaks hauled long-distance expresses from St Pancras after steam locomotives had been withdrawn. They were replaced with the introduction of the InterCity 125 in 1976. Peaks were powered with Swiss-designed Sulzer diesel engines.

The Midland Compound 4-4-0 was introduced in 1902 and designed by Richard Deeley (1855–1944). 240 of these locomotives were built, the last in 1932. Deeley was a pupil of Samuel Waite Johnson and succeeded him as Midland Locomotive Superintendent after his retirement.

A Midland passenger locomotive of 1866. Designed by Matthew Kirtley (1813–73), the first Midland Railway Locomotive Superintendent. He designed easily-maintained locomotives.

Thameslink, now First Capital Connect, Class 319 electric multiple unit trains were built between 1987 and 1988 for the renovated Thameslink route across London via Farringdon and Blackfriars. Power is supplied by 25-kilovolt, 50Hz AC overhead lines (north of Farringdon) and the 750-volt DC third rail system to the south.

Allegory: The Spirits of St Pancras
© Peter M Green GRA

Date	Structure	Architect	Ironmaster/engineer	Size of Structure	Comments
1781	Iron Bridge, Coalbrookdale, Shropshire	Thomas Pritchard (1723–77), architect	Abraham Darby (1750–91), ironmaster	Span 30.48m (100ft)	Designated a World Heritage site in 1987
1801–3	Pont des Arts, Paris, France		Louis-Alexandre de Cessart (1719–1806), and Jacques Lacrox-Dillon (1760–1807), engineers	Nine spans of 18.52m (60.76ft)	Rebuilt between 1981 and 1984 by Louis Gérald Attretche (1905–91) with seven spans
1824–30	Seyner Hütte Foundry, Bendorf, near Koblenz, Rhine, Germany	Karl Ludwig Althans (1788–1864), architect		Nave span of 7.85m (25.75ft), and side aisles 6.85m (22.47ft)	It is claimed that Karl Friedrich Schinkel (1780–1840) had some influence upon the design
1827–32	Chambre des Députés, Paris, France	Jules-Jean-Baptiste de Joly (1788–1865), architect		The ceiling, which has a maximum span of 67m (218ft), is suspended by a sophisticated iron structure.	The ceiling was painted by Delacroix
1844–48	The Palm House, Royal Botanic Gardens, Kew, London, England	Decimus Burton (1800–81), architect	Richard Turner (1798–1881), engineer and specialist in wrought- and cast-iron construction	Length 110m (362ft), width 30.48m (100ft), height 21m (69ft)	The most important surviving nineteenth-century iron and glass structure. The Royal Botanic Gardens were designated a World Heritage site in 2003
1844–49	Gare de l'Est, Paris, France	François-Alexandre Duquesney (1790–1849), architect	Pierre-Alexandre Cabanel de Sermet (1801–75), engineer	Span 29.72m (97ft)	Greatly admired by George Gilbert Scott
1851	The Great Exhibition Hall, Hyde Park, London, England		Sir Joseph Paxton, engineer	Barrel vault 21.94m (72ft)	Dismantled and re-erected, with modifications, at Sydenham, south London in 1854, where the Crystal Palace Company created a popular architectural museum. The structure as destroyed by fire in 1936
1852–54	Paddington station, London, England	Matthew Digby Wyatt (1820–77), and Owen Jones (1809–74), architects	Isambard Kingdom Brunel (1806–59), engineer	Major span 31m (102ft), subsidiary spans 14m (54ft)	'For detail of ornamentation I have neither time nor knowledge.' Brunel
1854	New Street station, Birmingham, England		Edward Alfred Cowper (1819–93), engineer	Span 64.31m (211ft)	Cowper was responsible for the contract drawings for Paxton's Great Exhibition building. George Gilbert Scott described Cowper's roof as 'wonderful'. Replaced by a new station building in the 1960s
1859–62	Gare d'Austerlitz, Paris, France		Leonce Reynaud (1803–80), engineer	Span 51m (167.32ft)	The vast internal space was used for the manufacture of passenger balloons during the Prussian siege of 1870

Date	Structure	Architect	Ironmaster/engineer	Size of Structure	Comments
1867–71	The Royal Albert Hall, Kensington Gore, London, England – cupola	Captain Francis Fowke (1823–65) and Henry Young Darracott Scott (1822–83), architects for the building	Rowland Mason Ordish (1824–86), and John William Groover, engineers for the cupola	Elliptical structure span 57–67m (187–218ft)	Ordish provided an elegant solution to a daunting structural problem. Not visible from the interior of the hall
1865–68	St Pancras station, London, England	Sir George Gilbert Scott (1811–78), architect for the station hotel and offices	William Henry Barlow (1812–1902) and Rowland Mason Ordish (1824–86), engineers for the train shed	Span 73.15m (240ft)	Until surpassed by the Palais des Machines in 1889 this was the largest single span structure. Its influence was immense throughout the industrialized world
1867–79	Lime Street station, Liverpool, England		William Baker (1817–78), and Francis Stevenson (1827–1902), engineers	Span 61m (200ft)	The earlier roof the station was designed by Richard Turner (1798–1881) – co-designer of the Palm House at Kew – and Sir William Fairburn (1789–1874)
1880–82	Victoria station, London, England		John Fowler (1817–98), engineer	Span 78m (256ft)	
1881	Pennsylvania Railroad Station, Broad Street and Market Street, Philadelphia, Pennsylvania, United States	Wilson Brothers & Company architects: Joseph Miller Wilson (1838–1902), John Allston Wilson (1837–1906) and Frederick Godfrey Thorn (fl. 1857–1911)		Span 91.44m (300ft)	The roof was destroyed by fire in 1923 and the station demolished in 1952
1885–87	Hauptbahnhof, Frankfurt-am-Main, Germany	Herrmann Eggert (1844–1920), and Johann Wilhelm Schwedler (1823–94), architects		3 principal spans of 56m (179.65ft)	One of the largest stations in the world
1889	Palais des Machines, Exposition Universelle, Paris, France	Charles-Louis-Ferdinand Dutert (1845–1906), architect	Victor Contamin (1840–93), engineer	Span 110.60m (362.86ft)	The first great steel structure. Demolished in 1909
1891–31	Reading Station, Philadelphia, Pennsylvania, United States	Francis Hatch Kimball (1845–1919) with the Wilson Brothers, architects (see also Pennsylvania Railroad Station, 1881)		Span 78.03m (256ft)	There are clear affinities with the structure of the St Pancras train shed
1893	World's Columbian Exhibition – Chicago World's Fair: Manufactures and Liberal Arts Building, United States	George B. Post (1837–1913), architect		Span 112.76m (370ft)	The largest enclosed space of the nineteenth century. However, it had far less impact on engineering practice than the Palais des Machines
1898	Dresden, Hauptbahnhof, Germany	Ernst Giese (1832–1903), architect and Arwed Rossbach (1844–1902), associated architect	Paul Weidner (1843–98), engineer	Principal span 59m (193.57ft)	A translucent skin of Teflon-coated glass fibre covers the original structure during station redevelopment by Foster + Partners between 1997 and 2006. Winner of the Institution of Structural Engineers' Heritage Award for Infrastructure 2007

Clients London & Continental Railways Ltd through subsidiary companies London & Continental Stations & Property Ltd and Union Railways (North) Ltd

Total cost £800 million
Masterplanner Foster + Partners

Basebuild Contract

Tender date 01 April 2001
Start on site date Phased access commencing 01 October 2001
Contract duration 6 years 3 months
Form of contract/procurement NEC Option C – Amended
Architect Rail Link Engineering (a consortium of Ove Arup & Partners, Bechtel Ltd, Sir William Halcrow & Partners Ltd and Systra)
Project Manager Rail Link Engineering
Trainshed Lighting Consultant Claude Engel III

Main Contractor Joint venture of Costain, Laing O'Rourke, Bachy Soletanche and Emcor Rail (Corber)

Selected subcontractors/suppliers

Conservation ironwork repairs Shepley Engineers Ltd
Conservation ironwork cleaning and painting SUI Generis
Conservation roof slating and leadwork T&P Roofing
Train shed roof glazing and end screens Pioneer
Conservation brickwork and stonework Paye, Stonewest
Conservation joinery Howard Brothers
Brickwork and stonework to rebuild west side buildings Irvine Whitlock
Decorative cast screens McNealy Brown
Structural steelwork (extension) Watson
Structural steelwork (east side building's roof) Lionweld Kennedy
North light glazing & transition roof Pioneer
Roof finishes Prater Roofing Ltd
Structural glazing Melaway
Rainwater disposal system Fullflow
Metalwork louvres McNealy Brown
Brickwork & blockwork Irvine Whitlock
Plaster, rendering, screeds and dry-lining Progressive
Suspended ceilings Thermofelt
Raised flooring Kingspan
Carpets & vinyl flooring Axiom Contract Flooring
Terrazzo & slate flooring W.B. Simpson
Ceramic tiling Wilson & Wylie
Doors Martin Roberts
Roller shutters Hart Door Systems

Toilet cubicles Thrislington
Structural glass assemblies Optima Architectural Glass
Cassetted wall cladding & booths Sorba
Decoration Sharrocks
Kitchen units Howard Brothers
Desks & counters Benbow
Ticket check-in booths Edmont
Booms, totem & Passenger Information Points installation Entech
Building Management Systems Johnson Controls

Thameslink Body Fitout Rail Link Engineering
Highways and Utilities Division Edmund Nuttall Ltd
Lifts Fujitec UK Ltd
Escalators Otis Ltd
Station Clock E. Dent & Co Ltd

King's Cross/St Pancras Underground Station

Client London Underground Ltd
Architects Arup with Allies & Morrison

St Pancras Chambers Development

Client Manhattan Loft Corporation
Architects RHWL
Richard Griffiths Associates

St Pancras Fit-Out Statistics

Start on site date Phased access: March 2007
Contract duration 10 months
Form of contract/procurement NEC 2/3 Cost reimbursable (Option 5)
Architects Chapman Taylor
Concept Design Arup Associates
Land Design
Input Group
Structural Engineer Lucking and Clarke
Planning Supervisor/Construction Design Safety Works
Managers Co-ordinator Security Consultant Arup Security
Fire Strategy Consultant Arup Fire
Corporate and retail signage Transport Design Consultancy
Project Manager Bechtel

Fit-Out

Main Contractor ISG

Selected subcontractors/suppliers

Builders' work Mountfield Building Group

Staircase – Business Premier Lounge

  Glazzard (Dudley) Ltd

Glazed shop fronts, glazed partitioning, roller shutters

  Optima Architectural Glass

Brickwork Stonewest Ltd

Drylining & firestopping London Drywall

Specialist ceilings Phoenix Interiors Ltd

Specialist ceilings – Business Premier Lounge

  Carlton Ceilings & Partitions

Raised access floor & ceramic tiling

  Connaught Access Flooring

Terrazzo Matthew Stone Restoration Co Ltd

Joinery Taylor Made Joinery

  Benbow Interiors

  Brown & Carroll

Floor finishes Wayment Flooring Specialists

Timber flooring Loughton Contract Carpets

Architectural metalwork PAD Contracts Ltd

Decorations H&S Decorating Specialists Ltd

Window blinds – Business Premier Lounge

  Timorous Beasties

Signage Blaze Neon Ltd

Specialist signage – Passenger Information Points

  Wood & Wood

Specialist signage Doric

Mechanical & Electrical Plant installations

  Spie Matthew Hall Ltd

Closed Circuit Television Siemens Building Technologies

Public Address/Voice Alarm Sysco

Data cabling Comunica

Commissioning Core Group Ltd

Selected Building Services: Subcontractors/Suppliers

Passenger Information Points & Booms

  Environmental Technology

Building management Johnson Control Systems

Ductwork Senior Hargreaves

Sprinklers & fire protection Wormald Ansul (Tyco)

Insulation – Mechanical & Electrical

  Western Thermal Limited

Data Networking specialist labour LTE Network Communications Ltd

Station control system Application Solutions Ltd

Flush & chemical clean mechanical pipework

  PH Water Technologies Ltd

Vacuum drainage Kylemore Services

Mechanical commissioning Moores Commissioning Services Ltd

Mains cable installation FB Taylor Cable

Closed Circuit Television Installation & testing

  Install CCTV Limited

Emergency Access Control System/Intruder Detection System

  Honeywell Ltd

Customer information system Transmitton Limited

Chillers – Air Toshiba Carrier UK Limited

Telephone Exchange Switch Communications Ltd

Air conditioning – Static installation

  Set Point Air Conditioning

Communications – Data Transmitton Limited

Car park ventilation Colt International

DX air conditioning system CRT Commissioning

Trench heating HCP

Fan coil unit installation RDS

Relocation of Substation (Mechanical and Electrical Plant)

  Instrument & Control Services

Telecommunications survey AMS Acoustics Limited

Erection, testing & commissioning Low Voltage Panels

  Lounsdale Electrical

Lightning protection RC Cutting & Co.

Structured cabling Switch Communications Ltd

Aspirating systems (air sampling) Advanced Commercial Installations Ltd

  Install PIS enclosure Tegrel Ltd

Busbar installation Zucchini Busbar UK Ltd

Closed Circuit Television infrastructure

  Controlware GMBH

Terminate & testing fibre optic cables

  EMCOR Facilities Services

Low Voltage Panel modifications Lounsdale Electrical

Oil monitoring system Aquasentry Ltd

RAILWAY ARCHITECTURE

MEEKS, Caroll L. V. *The Railroad Station*. New Haven and London: Yale University Press, 1956 – later republished by Castle Books, New York, 1978.

Carroll Meeks (1907–66) taught architecture at Yale. Impressive in its scholarship, this is still the standard work on the subject. Meeks' Bibliographical Essay is of great importance in the study of the station as a building type.

THE CHANNEL TUNNEL

GOURVISH, T. R. *The official history of Britain and the Channel Tunnel*. London: Routledge, 2006.

The standard work.

ST PANCRAS STATION and the MIDLAND and ASSOCIATED RAILWAYS

BARLOW, Peter (1776–1862) – the father of W. H. Barlow) *A treatise on the strength of timber, cast iron, malleable iron, and other materials; with rules for application in architecture, construction of suspension bridges, railways, etc. with an appendix, on the power of locomotive engines*. London: John Weale, Architectural Library, 1837.

BARLOW, W. H. Appendix to the Paper of Mr. W. H. Barlow, on an 'Element of Strength in Beams Subjected to Transverse Strain, &c.' [Abstract]. *Proceedings of the Royal Society of London, Vol. 8, 1856–1857,* p. 442.

BARLOW, W. H. 'Description of the St Pancras Station and Roof, Midland Railway.' Paper read to Institution of Civil Engineers, 29 March, 1870, Minutes of the Proceedings of the Institution of Civil Engineers, 1870.

This is the most important contemporary account of the construction of the St Pancras train shed. Barlow observes: 'For the details of the roof the author is indebted to Mr Ordish, whose practical knowledge and excellent suggestions enabled him, while adhering to the form, depth and general design, to effect many improvements in its construction.'

– BARLOW, W. H. 'On the construction of permanent way of railways; with an account of the wrought-iron permanent way ... on the ... Midland Railway.' Paper read to the Institution of Civil Engineers, 14 May, 1850, Minutes of the Proceedings of the Institution of Civil Engineers, London 1850.

– BARLOW, W. H. 'On the roof of St Pancras station.' *Proceedings of the RIBA (1870–71),* pp. 117–30.

– BARLOW, W. H. 'Presidential address to the Institution of Civil Engineers.' Minutes of the Proceedings of the Institution of Civil Engineers, 1880, pp. 2–23.

(BARLOW, W. H.) BUCK, George Watson *A practical and theoretical essay on oblique bridges… revised by J Watson Buck and with addition of description to diagrams for facilitating the construction of oblique bridges by W. H. Barlow*. London: Crosby Lockwood, 1895.

(BARLOW, W. H.) LEWIS, C. 'William Henry Barlow, 1812–1902'. *Back Track*, Vol. 20, No. 7, July 2006, pp. 402–410.

(BARLOW, W. H. and ORDISH, R. M.) *Works in iron by Andrew Handyside & Co., Britannia Iron Works, Derby, and 32, Walbrook, London*. London: E. & F. Spon, 1868.

Barlow and R. M. Ordish were both closely associated with Handyside & Co. – although Ewing Matheson, 1840–1917, appears to have been the company's in-house designer. Ordish's design for the train shed of Amsterdam station, for the Dutch Rhenish Railway (1862), is illustrated here, together with a large reception hall for India that he designed in collaboration with Owen Jones. Illustrated by photographs.

(BARLOW, W. H. and ORDISH, R. M.) MATHESON, Ewing *Works in Iron. Bridge and roof structures, with examples of structures made and erected by Andw. Handyside & Co., Derby and London, 1877*. London: E. & F. N. Spon, 1877.

Contains details and illustrations of Ordish's designs for a bridge at Czernowitz, Bukowina, the Albert Bridge, Chelsea, and the Winter Garden at Leeds Infirmary, which he designed with Gilbert Scott.

BARNARD, Simon (author and illustrator) *The Dragon of St Pancras*. London: Rex Collings, 1971.

An eccentric tale of an invisible dragon set in St Pancras station. Significantly, the dragon is called 'Beeching'.

BARNES, E. G. *The Midland main line 1875–1922*. London: George Allen & Unwin Ltd, 1969.

This is the standard work. The author deals with every aspect of the railway and is especially interesting on locomotive design – of which the Midland Railway was justifiably proud. See also following entry.

– BARNES, E. G. *The rise of the Midland Railway, 1844–74*. London: George Allen & Unwin Ltd, 1966.

ALAN BAXTER & ASSOCIATES *Planning & listed building submission. Conservation plan.* Prepared by Alan Baxter & Associates. 2 July 2004, London: Alan Baxter & Associates, 2004.

For private circulation. Primarily concerned with the re-use of Scott's Midland Grand Hotel. A model document that contains much useful contextual information. (RHWL Architects, Richard Griffiths Architects, Alan Baxter & Associates, Arup, Faber Maunsell, Jeremy Gardner and Associates, AYH.)

BETJEMAN, John and GAY, John (photographs) *London's historic railway stations*. London: John Murray, 1972.

See pp. 10–21 for 'St Pancras – the best published photographic survey of St Pancras before its present transformation.' Gay's photographs are now in the possession of the Royal Institute of British Architects.

BRADLEY, Simon *St Pancras Station*. London: Profile Books Ltd, 2007.

Admirable in its range of themes. In the Wonders of the World series.

CHASSEAUD, Peter *King's Cross*. Lewes, East Sussex: Altazimuth Press, 2004.

An artist's book published in a limited edition of 50. It includes photographs – some by the author, some from archival sources. Good photographs of St Pancras.

CHRISTIAN, Roy *Butterley Brick, 200 years in the making*. London: Henry Melland, 1990.

See Chapter 6 – the Butterley company was responsible for the construction of the St Pancras train shed arch ribs.

(COWPER, Edward Alfred) *Obituary of Edward Alfred Cowper (1819–93),* Journal of the Institution of Civil Engineers, 1893

Cowper was the designer of the magnificent wrought-iron and glass roof of Birmingham New Street station – at nearly 65m, the largest single span in the world until surpassed by Barlow's and Ordish's St Pancras train shed roof at 74m.

CRUIKSHANK, Dan and PARKER, John *The story of Britain's best buildings*. London: BBC Worldwide, 2002.

Includes the Midland Grand Hotel, St Pancras.

DOW, George *Midland style*. London, Bromley: Historical Model Railway Society, 1975.

Intended for railway modellers – contains colour swatches.

GREATER LONDON COUNCIL *King's Cross and St Pancras, GLC action area draft local plan*. London: GLC, 1985.

'Approved by the Planning Committee, Greater London Council, on 26 June 1985, for the purposes of consultation.'

JACKSON, Alan A. *London's termini*. Newton Abbot, Devon: David & Charles, 1969.

Includes chapters on Euston, St Pancras and King's Cross, and a useful bibliography.

JONES, Charles Henry *The Midland Railway locomotive works*. With illustrations from photographs by Mr Scotton, the Company's official photographer. London: from an as yet unidentified journal.

LACY, R. E. and DOW, George *Midland Railway carriages*. Berkshire: Wild Swan, 1984.

The Midland Counties Railway Companion, with topographical descriptions of the country and time, fare and distance tables and complete guides to London & Birmingham and Birmingham & Derby Junction Railways. Derby: R & F Allen, 1840.

NEVILLE, R. and MACNAMARA, H. and others *Reports of cases decided by the Railway Commissioners: Railway and canal traffic cases*. London: Sweet and Maxwell, 1874–1938.

There were numerous cases of litigation relating to the bridging of canals in the nineteenth century.

ORDISH, R. M. and MATHESON, Ewing *Proposed bridge over the Thames by the Tower*. London: 1885.

A lithographic plate, together with descriptive text, in the Library of the Institution of Civil Engineers. This apparently relates to the following item.

ORDISH R. M. (attributed) *Design for a suspension bridge over the Thames*.

The watercolour and bodycolour design is dated from between 1863 and 1865. The size is 73 x 253cm and is a typical client presentation illustration of the era. The proposed bridge was to be situated east of St Paul's and apparently close to Thomas Telford's St Katharine's Dock and very close to the site of the present Tower Bridge. Although the bridge is described as a 'railway suspension bridge' by the Art Fund, the span appears too great for railway traffic and has a curvature, which would make it unsuitable for railway use. Ordish is known for his interest in suspension bridges. The illustration is in the Guildhall Library, City of London.

PEVSNER, Nikolaus *The Buildings of England: London, except the Cities of London and Westminster*. Harmondsworth, Middlesex: Penguin Books, 1952.

PHILLIPS *Railway map of the British Isles showing the new grouping system*. London: Phillips, 1927.

This shows all the routes of the London, Midland & Scottish Railway – which incorporated the Midland Railway's lines after the re-grouping of 1922.

RADFORD, J. B. *The Derby works and Midland locomotives*. Shepperton, Middlesex: Ian Allan Ltd, 1971.

 – RADFORD *Midland Line memories: a pictorial history of the Midland Railway main line between London (St Pancras) and Derb*. London: Bloomsbury Books, 1983.

ROLT, L. T. C. *George and Robert Stephenson: The railway revolution*. London: Longmans, 1960.

The Stephensons, father and son, played an important part in the early history of the Midland Railway.

SIMMONS, Jack *St Pancras Station*. London: Historical Publications, 1968 and revised and with an additional chapter by Robert Thorne in 2003.

SMITHSON, Alison and Peter *The Euston Arch and the growth of the London, Midland and Scottish Railway*. London: Thames & Hudson, 1968.

Besides being the best account of the wanton destruction of the Euston Arch by British Railways this is among the finest visual evocations of the great railway age. Foreword by Nikolaus Pevsner.

STAMP, Gavin and AMERY, Colin *Victorian Buildings of London: an illustrated guide*. London: The Architectural Press, 1982.

St Pancras is dealt with in some detail.

STEPHENSON, George *Map of the North Midland Railway and adjacent country*. George Stephenson, engineer: no town of publication, no publisher, no date (c.1840).

A large folding map mounted on canvas – 208cm (82 in) x 132cm (52 in).

The map shows a number of the smaller railways, which were to be incorporated later into the Midland Railway system. These are Liverpool and Manchester Railway (1830), Bolton and Leigh Railway (1831), Warrington and Newton Railway (1831), Leicester and Swannington Railway (1831), Midland Counties Railway (1832), Leeds and Selby Railway (1834), Preston and Wyre Railway (1835), Great North of England Railway (1836), Birmingham and Gloucester Railway (1836), Grand Junction Railway (1837), Manchester and Bolton Railway (1838), Sheffield and Rotherham Railway (1838), Chester and Crewe Railway – which was absorbed by the Grand Junction Railway in 1840. George Stephenson (1781–1848), 'the father of the railway' and his son Robert Stephenson (1803–59) were responsible for surveying several of these projects.

STEPHENSON, Robert *Presidential address to the Institution of Civil Engineers, January 8, 1856*. Journal of the Institution of Civil Engineers, 1856 (pp. 123–54).

(STEPHENSON, Robert) (Anonymous) *Obituary of Robert Stephenson (1803–59)*. Journal of the Institution of Civil Engineers, 1859 (pp. 176–82).

STRETTON, Clement E. *The history of the Midland Railway*. London: Methuen & Co., 1901.

SWENSEN, Steven P. *Mapping Poverty in Agar Town: Economic Conditions prior to the development of St Pancras Station in 1866*. Published by London School of Economics, Department of Economic History, June 2006.

This study was published as part of 'Working Papers on The Nature of Evidence: How Well Do 'Facts' Travel?' No. 09/06. It highlighted the apparent welcome that was given to the eradication of very poor housing initially without any arrangements being made to house those dispossessed. The Midland Railway was, when developing the Somers Town goods depot, forced to provide alternative housing.

VIGNOLES, Charles Blacker *Map of that portion of the Midland Counties Railway extending from its junction with the London and Birmingham Railway at Rugby to the North side of the River Trent and between Nottingham and Derby. Constructed upon the Trigonometrical Points of the Ordnance Survey of Great Britain furnished by permission of the Right Honourable The Board of Ordnance by Captain Robe R.E. The whole from Surveys made under the immediate Directions and Superintendence of Charles Vignoles, Civil Engineer, London, engraved by J. Gardner, Regent Street*. No date (c. 1835).

A folding map mounted on canvas – 95cm (37½in) x 65cm (25½in).

The Midland Counties Railway was to become a major part of the Midland Railway. Charles Blacker Vignoles (1793–1875) was one of the most important early railway surveyors. He was born in Wexford, Ireland. Orphaned in childhood he was brought up by his grandfather who was Professor of Mathematics at the Royal Military Academy, Woolwich. He was commissioned in the army and served with Lord Wellington. Later, he surveyed parts of the southern United States. He conducted early railway surveys in Germany and the Ukraine – then Russia. Vignoles was first Professor of Civil Engineering at University College, London and President of the Institution of Civil Engineers in 1869.

VIOLLET-LE-DUC, E. E. (principal editor) *Encyclopédie d'architecture. Revue mensuelle*. Paris: A. Morel, 1872–77.

Contains excellent engravings of a section and side elevation of Barlow's and Ordish's train shed.

WALKER, James and RASTRICK, John Urpeth *Liverpool and Manchester Railway. Report to the Directors on the comparative merits of locomotive and fixed engines, as a moving ppower*. Liverpool: printed by Wales and Baines, 1829.

For a time, trains rope-hauled by stationary engines were contemplated. Robert Stephenson was strongly opposed to stationary engines.

WARREN, John Cecil Turnbull *Conservation of brick*… Oxford: Butterworth-Heinemann, 1999.

With a contribution by Pat Ryan and David Andrews. From the Butterworth-Heinemann series in conservation and museology, includes a case study of St Pancras Station.

WILLIAMS, Frederick S. *The Midland Railway: Its rise and progress: A narrative of modern enterprise*. London and Irongate (Derby): Bemrose & Co, 1877.

The standard contemporary account.

WILLIAMS, R. *The Midland Railway: A New History,* Newton Abbot, Devon: David and Charles, 1988.

Sir GEORGE GILBERT SCOTT

SCOTT, Sir George Gilbert *Design for the new law courts submitted by Geo. Gilbert Scott, R.A.* London: Day, 1867.

– SCOTT *Lectures on the rise and development of medieval architecture delivered at the Royal Academy* (2 volumes). London: John Murray,1879.

The lectures began in 1855. Illustrated with 456 fine wood-engravings. One of the last great books on medieval architecture by a practising architect.

– SCOTT *On the Conservation of Ancient Architectural Monuments and remains.* London: 1864.

A 36 pp. pamphlet.

– SCOTT *Personal and professional recollections: by the late Sir George Gilbert Scott.* Edited by his son G. Gilbert Scott. London: Sampson Low, Marston, Searle, & Rivington, 1879.

An introduction by the Very Rev. John William Burgon. The work was re-published in 1995 by Paul Watkins, of Stamford, Lincolnshire, as a facsimile edition. It was edited by Gavin Stamp and is of far greater documentary importance than the original edition – it contains, for example, material thought to be too personal, or libellous, which Scott's son had excluded from his father's diaries. Stamp's introduction is admirable and his appendices and index render the work an excellent substitute for the fully-fledged modern biographical treatment, which William Burges, William Butterfield, George Devey, A. W. N. Pugin, Anthony Salvin, Richard Norman Shaw and Philip Webb have received.

– SCOTT *Remarks on secular and domestic architecture, present and future.* London: John Murray, 1857.

This is among the most important theoretical texts by a nineteenth century architect. Scott emerges not as a narrow medievaliser but as an enthusiast for progress. Chapter IX – on Commercial Buildings – contains many observations on railway architecture, which evidently interested him greatly.

– SCOTT *A plea for the faithful restoration of our ancient churches: a paper read before the Architectural and Archaeological Society for the County of Bucks, at their first annual meeting in 1848. To which are added some miscellaneous remarks on other subjects connected with the restoration of churches, and the revival of pointed architecture.* London: Parker, 1850.

(SCOTT) *The Albert Memorial, the National Memorial to His Royal Highness the Prince Consort.* London: John Murray, 1873.

The definitive account of the memorial in Kensington Gardens – once derided and now admired.

(SCOTT) (Anonymous) *St Pancras Chambers, formerly the Midland Grand Hotel.* London: London & Continental Stations Property Ltd (1999).

A publicity brochure commemorating the restoration of the Midland Grand Hotel.

(SCOTT) BRITTON, John and PEACH, R. E. M. *The history and antiquities of Bath Abbey Church by John Britton. Continued to the present time, with additional notes by R. E. M. Peach, Bath.* Charles Halbert and London: Adams & Co, 1887.

Bath Abbey is one of the finer examples of the Perpendicular style. Scott's restoration work went on for ten years from 1864. 'Under the able hand of Sir George Gilbert Scott, and at a very large cost, this venerable Abbey has resumed its pristine beauty…'

(SCOTT) CLARK, Kenneth *The Gothic Revival. An essay in the history of taste.* London: Constable & Co. Ltd, 1928 (there have been numerous reprints of the third edition, 1962, published by John Murray).

See Chapter IX. It is significant in this pioneering historiography of the Gothic Revival that Clark chooses the careers of A. W. N. Pugin and Scott as test cases.

(SCOTT) COLE, David *The work of Sir Gilbert Scott.* London: Architectural Press, 1980.

Contains an extensive bibliography.

(SCOTT) CROOK, J. Mordaunt *The dilemma of style: architectural ideas from the picturesque to the post modern.* London: John Murray, 1987.

Contains numerous references to Scott. Particularly useful in placing him within the context of architectural debate in his era.

(SCOTT) DIXON, Roger and MUTHESIUS, Stefan *Victorian Architecture*, London: Thames & Hudson, 1978 (second edition 1985, reprinted 1988).

With a short dictionary of architects.

(SCOTT) FERRIDAY, Peter (editor) *Victorian Architecture.* London: Jonathan Cape, 1968.

With an introduction by John Betjeman and contributions by Nikolaus Pevsner, Frank Jenkins, H. S. Goodhart Rendel, E. M. Dodd, Peter Fleetwood-Hesketh, Alexandra Gordon Clark, Robert Furneaux Jordan, Paul Thompson, David Cole, Charles Handley-Read, Joseph Kinnard, John Brandon-Jones and Halsey Ricardo.

See David Cole on Sir George Gilbert Scott (pp. 177–86)

(SCOTT) FURNEAUX JORDAN, Robert *Victorian Architecture.* Harmondsworth: Penguin Books, 1966.

Robert Furneaux Jordan (1905–78) was for a time Principal of the Architectural Association School of Architecture – the flagship of British modernism. His views on Victorian architecture are representative of the change in attitudes that began with the writings of Nikolaus Pevsner and the enthusiasms of John Betjeman. Furneaux Jordan writes, 'The St Pancras Hotel … is most likely to be regarded as a symbol, not only of Scott himself, but of the whole mid-Victorian epoch. It combines in one building the romantic aspirations, the stylistic display and the solid philistinism of the sixties. With its variegated and strident materials, its tremendously Gothic skyline and its ramped and terraced base, it is a most positive piece of design not a mere essay in the Gothic style.' (See pp. 92–7 for a discussion of Scott.)

(SCOTT) PEVSNER, Nikolaus *The buildings of England: Nottinghamshire*. Harmondsworth: Penguin Books, 1951.

See Kelham Hall, a house of which Scott was particularly proud and which influenced his design of the Midland Grand Hotel.

(SCOTT) SAVILLE, J. 'London: St Pancras Station Hotel; Architects: Sir G. Gilbert-Scott'. *Building News*, 1874, (1) pp. 283, 554, plates pp. 558–59.

J. Saville appears to have been John Saville Wright, Clerk of the Works.

(SCOTT) SCOTT, Francis Edward, Sir *Shall the new foreign office be Gothic or Classic? A plea for the former: addressed to the Members of the House of Commons.* London: Bell and Daldy, 1860.

An intelligent defence of Scott's choice of an Italian Gothic style for the Foreign Office. In the event, Scott was obliged to compromise and a building in the sixteenth century Italian Renaissance style was the outcome.

(SCOTT) Sir George Gilbert Scott (1811–78 March 27), R.A., F.S.A., P.R.I.B.A. (1873–76) 'A list of his works (buildings and writings) and a bibliography, based on published material.' London: Royal Institute of British Architects, 1957.

Typescript – 90 pp.

EXHIBITIONS devoted to the work of Sir GEORGE GILBERT SCOTT
George Gilbert Scott, 1811–78: architect

Newark, Newark Museum and Art Gallery (Nottinghamshire, England), August–September 1978.

3 pp. catalogue of a small exhibition held at the Museum and Art Gallery, Newark-upon-Trent.

Sir Gilbert Scott (1811–78): Architect of the Gothic Revival.

London: The Victoria & Albert Museum, 1978.

A 32 pp catalogue of an exhibition (31 May–10 September 1978) containing a short biography of Scott, and essays by David Cole – 'The Buildings', S. E. Dykes Bower – 'The Restoration of the Cathedrals' and Gavin Stamp – 'The Office and Heirs of Sir Gilbert Scott.'

EXHIBITIONS in which the work of SCOTT featured prominently
PHYSICK, John and DARBY, Michael '*Marble Halls.'* Drawings and models for Victorian secular buildings.*

London: HMSO, 1973.

Catalogue of an exhibition held at the Victoria & Albert Museum, August–October 1973. Of Scott's buildings which were shown were: the Foreign Office (1867), the Midland Grand Hotel (1865–77) and the National Memorial in Kensington Gardens to the Prince Consort (model c.1863). Of considerable interest is also the unpremiated design by Owen Jones (1809–74) for the Midland Grand Hotel. Jones was the only architect among the entrants in the Midland Grand Hotel design competition to exploit the grandeur of Barlow's train shed.

Victorian Church Art, Exhibition (November 1971–January 1972)

London, Victoria & Albert Museum, 1971.

Section F was devoted entirely to Scott.

The authors and URN thank the sources of photographs for supplying and granting permission to reproduce them. Every effort has been made to contact all copyright holders, but should there be any errors or omissions URN would be pleased to insert the appropriate acknowledgement in any subsequent printing of this publication.

Allies and Morrison 144 (bottom right)

Anderson-Terzic 172–173

Arup 144 (bottom right)

Associated Book Publishers Ltd. (The History of the Midland Railway by C E Stretton) 18 (bottom right)

BRB Residuary Ltd 221 (top right, middle centre, and bottom left); 222 (far right); 223 (bottom left)

Camden Local Studies and Archives Centre (endpapers); 14 (top and bottom); 37 (bottom right); 176 (top); 219 (bottom left)

Camera Press 221 (bottom right)

Chapman Taylor 56 (middle); 57 (centre and bottom); 59 (bottom); 198; 200 (bottom)

Childs, Paul (cover); 7; 10; 26–27; 28; 29; 30–31; 32; 33; 34; 34–35; 35; 36; 37 (top and bottom left); 38; 39; 40 (top left and bottom right); 41; 42; 43; 44; 45; 46; 47; 48; 49; 53 (top and middle); 54; 55 (top); 56 (top and bottom); 59 (top); 62–63; 64 (top left; bottom left and centre); 66; 67; 68; 69; 70; 70–71; 71; 72; 72–73; 74; 75; 76; 77 (bottom); 78; 79; 80–81; 82 (top, centre and bottom left); 83; 84 (centre left; bottom left and right); 85; 86; 87; 88; 89; 90; 91; 92; 93; 94; 95; 96; 97; 98–99; 100 (top); 103 (bottom left and right); 104; 105; 106–107; 107 (top right); 108; 110; 110–111; 111; 112; 113; 114 (bottom right); 115; 116; 116–117; 117; 118; 119; 120–121; 122 (bottom left and right); 123 (top left); 124; 127; 128 (top); 129; 130–131; 132; 133; 134 (top left); 135 (bottom left and right); 136 (bottom); 137; 138; 138–139; 139; 140; 146 (bottom); 147; 148–149; 148; 149; 152; 153; 154; 155; 156–157; 158 (left); 159; 162 (right); 164; 165; 174 (top); 175 (bottom); 182–183; 184–185; 186–187; 188; 189; 190–191; 191; 192–193; 193; 194; 196; 197; 199; 200 (top); 201; 202 (bottom); 203; 204 (top); 205; 207; 208–209; 213; 214–215; 216 (top)

Chung, Dan 82 (bottom right)

Cossons, Sir Neil 6

Cowlard, David 107 (top left)

Dalton Maag 195

David and Charles (publishers of The Midland Railway by Frederick Smeeton William) 176 (centre); 219 (bottom centre)

Department for Transport, The 222 (top left); 224 (top left)

Emmwood 25 (bottom)

English Heritage 103 (top)

Eurostar UK 224 (bottom left); 225 (bottom left)

Evans, Mary see Mary Evans

Eye Ubiquitous 202 (top)

Gambrill, Bernard 219 (top 2 images); 221 (middle right)

Getty Images 206 (bottom)

Getty/Hulton 12 (bottom right); 13; 16 (top); 20 (bottom left); 21 (bottom); 163 (bottom); 175 (top)

GMJ 178; 180; 181 (top)

Green, Peter 53 (bottom); 226–227

Griffiths, Richard Architects see Richard Griffiths Architects

Guardian 82 (bottom right)

Guildhall Library 177 (top)

Historical Model Railway Society 220 (top right)

Historical Publications (St Pancras Station by Jack Simmons, 2003) 160 (right)

Hulton Getty 102 (centre); 221 (top left)

Illustrated London News 16 (centre); 177 (bottom)

Institute of Civil Engineers 22 (top and bottom left); 23; 218

Kaukas, Bernard 222 (centre)

Kennet, Lord 222 (bottom left)

Logan, Iain 220 (bottom right)

London and Continental Railways 57 (top); 204 (bottom); 224 (top and bottom centre; top far right); 225 (centre; bottom far right)

LSE, Department of Economic History 174 (bottom)

Lycett Green, Candida 206 (top)

MacDonald, Eddie 210; 211; 212; 216 (bottom); 217; 225 (top far right)

Manhattan Lofts 167

Mary Evans Picture Library 16 (centre); 170 (left); 177 (bottom); 220 (top and bottom centre)

Midland Railway Society 220 (top left)

Miller Hare 181 (bottom)

Milner, Chris 225 (top left)

Motco Enterprises Ltd 14 (centre)

Museum of London (Frontispiece)

National 61 (right); 114 (bottom left)

National Archives, The 17 (top and bottom); 24 (bottom); 109 (top left); 114 (top left); 169 (bottom)

National Media Museum 102 (centre); 221 (top left)

National Portrait Gallery, London 21 (top)

National Railway Museum 12 (bottom left); 15 (top left; bottom left and right); 16 (bottom); 18 (top left; centre and bottom left); 19 (top left); 22 (bottom right); 40 (bottom left); 65 (top); 101 (right); 134 (centre left); 136 (top); 162 (centre and bottom); 163 (top and centre); 219 (top centre; far right); 221 (bottom centre)

Network Rail 150; 151

New Civil Engineer 52

NMR 103 (top)

O'Connor, John (frontispiece)

Punch 25 (bottom)

Quickbird Products 179

RCAHMS 168 (top)

RIBA Drawings and Archives Collections 158 (right); 160 (left); 161 (left); 162 (top)

Richard Griffiths Architects 170–171

Royal Windsor, The website 24 (top)

Science Museum 20 (top left)

Scott, George Gilbert (Medieval Architecture) 169 (top)

Shelton, Rod 64 (bottom right); 65 (bottom); 84 (top left); 102 (bottom); 109 (top right, bottom left and right); 122 (top left); 123 (bottom right); 125 (top and centre); 126; 128 (bottom left and right); 130 (top); 131 (top); 134 (bottom right); 166 (right)

Simmons Aerofilms 176 (bottom)

Snowden 221 (bottom right)

SSPL 12 (bottom left); 15 (top left; bottom left and right); 16 (bottom); 18 (top left; centre and bottom left); 19 (top left); 20 (top left); 22 (bottom right); 40 (bottom left); 65 (top); 101 (right); 102 (centre); 134 (centre left); 136 (top); 162 (centre and bottom); 163 (top and centre); 176 (bottom); 219 (top centre; far right); 221 (top left; bottom centre)

Swenson, Steven 174 (bottom)

Thomas Telford 52

Topfoto 61 (right); 114 (bottom left); 221 (top centre)

Townshend Landscape Architects 179

Transport Design 58

Transport for London 142; 144 (top and bottom left); 145; 146 (top)

Troika 50–51; 77 (top); 125 (bottom)

Union Railways 55 (middle and bottom); 60–61; 223 (centre; top and bottom far right); 224 (bottom right)

UPP 221 (top centre)

Urban Exposure 107 (top left)

Walter, Michael 50–51; 77 (top); 125 (bottom)

Willis, Ray 166 (left)

Yates, Ian 202 (top)

Index

Text Credit

The poetry by John Betjeman on page 207 is reproduced by permission of John Murray (Publishers) Limited.

Author's Acknowledgements

My thanks are due to Union Railways (North) Ltd and in particular Alan Dyke, former Managing Director. I also wish to thank Sir Neil Cossons, Chairman of English Heritage 2000–07, for his words of endorsement regarding the remarkable partnership between English Heritage, London Borough of Camden and London & Continental Railways. Thanks are also due to Royden Stock for his assistance in providing access to the former Midland Grand Hotel building. I am especially grateful for contributions by Peter William Davies, Stuart Durant, Alan Dyke, Bernard Gambrill and Roderick Shelton. As technical editor, Bernard Gambrill has been the linchpin responsible for the successful completion of this project. I would also like to thank Philip Cooper and Susie May at Laurence King Publishing for their professionalism and patience in the preparation of this book. Finally, I must thank my wife, Ayse, who has spent many hours supporting and encouraging me in the preparation of this book. Any faults are mine. I look forward to incorporating any necessary changes in a future edition.

Alastair Lansley